Walking
INTO MY
Freedom

Became more Than Just
Letting Go of My Past, it was
Finding my Identity

COLANDRA HALL

WESTBOW
PRESS®
A DIVISION OF THOMAS NELSON
& ZONDERVAN

This book is a work of non-fiction. Unless otherwise noted, the author and the publisher make no explicit guarantees as to the accuracy of the information contained in this book and in some cases, names of people and places have been altered to protect their privacy.

WestBow Press books may be ordered through booksellers or by contacting:

WestBow Press
A Division of Thomas Nelson & Zondervan
1663 Liberty Drive
Bloomington, IN 47403
www.westbowpress.com
844-714-3454

Because of the dynamic nature of the Internet, any web addresses or links contained in this book may have changed since publication and may no longer be valid. The views expressed in this work are solely those of the author and do not necessarily reflect the views of the publisher, and the publisher hereby disclaims any responsibility for them.

Any people depicted in stock imagery provided by Getty Images are models, and such images are being used for illustrative purposes only. Certain stock imagery © Getty Images.

Unless otherwise noted, all scripture comes from the King James Version of the Bible.

Scripture quotations marked (NIV) are taken from the Holy Bible, New International Version®, NIV®. Copyright © 1973, 1978, 1984, 2011 by Biblica, Inc.® Used by permission of Zondervan. All rights reserved worldwide. www.zondervan.com The "NIV" and "New International Version" are trademarks registered in the United States Patent and Trademark Office by Biblica, Inc.®

ISBN: 978-1-6642-2497-1 (sc)
ISBN: 978-1-6642-2496-4 (e)

Print information available on the last page.

WestBow Press rev. date: 03/04/2021

To my husband and our wonderful children.
Thank you for all your love and support throughout my
journey to freedom. You guys have cheered me on with
much patience and understanding. I love you guys.

Praise be to the God and Father of our Lord Jesus Christ! In his great mercy he has given us new birth into a living hope through the resurrection of Jesus Christ from the dead, and into an inheritance that can never perish, spoil or fade. This inheritance is kept in heaven for you, who through faith are shielded by God's power until the coming of the salvation that is ready to be revealed in the last time. In all this you greatly rejoice, through now for a little while you may have had to suffer grief in all kinds of trials. These have come so that the proven genuineness of your faith—of greater worth than gold, which perishes even though refined by fire—may result in praise, glory and honor when Jesus Christ is revealed.

—1 Peter 1:3–7 (NIV)

CONTENTS

Acknowledgments...vii

Preface xiii

Introduction xv

Chapter 1 How I Learned to Run Away.................................1
Chapter 2 Coming to Christ 12
Chapter 3 Fighting for Our Home 23
Chapter 4 Best Days Turned into Darkness........................34
Chapter 5 You're Going to Make It 46
Chapter 6 Keeping the Faith 53
Chapter 7 Coming Full Circle in My Life............................59
Chapter 8 No More Running 66
Chapter 9 Deliverance..73
Chapter 10 Separating Yourself..79

PREFACE

As I wrote this book, I was reminded of our Lord Jesus Christ and how he came into this world to save us. His plan has always been to restore us from our lives of sin and to welcome us into his family. God's love is so beautiful and full of joy, peace, and gentleness. We don't have to be afraid of receiving the gift of Christ. Though I've longed for Christ's love in my past, it wasn't out of my reach. I just couldn't see it in the way that Christ was showing it to me. Instead of receiving Christ's invitation, I took in Christ's love only when I needed it. If I thought I was good with my life, I would walk away from it until I needed it again. I did this for years until Christ showed me myself. I knew then that I needed Christ in my life every day. So, I stopped running away from Christ and ran to him, and he has been with me ever since that day. I knew I wouldn't have made it in this world without him. My prayer is that someone who is struggling with their faith will come to know the Lord as their Savior, Redeemer, strong tower, peace, love, healer, way maker, Counselor—the list of qualities that Jesus offers in exchange for our sins goes on into eternity.

On a final note, unless otherwise stated, all scripture references in this book are taken from the King James Version of the Bible.

God bless you all. Amen.

INTRODUCTION

In 2001, God called me by my name daughter, warrior, teacher, and Colandra, but I did not know that he was also calling me to a place of rest, peace, and joy. Years passed, and there came trouble. I was defenseless because I did not know who I was in Christ Jesus. Even though God knew me by name, I didn't know my true identity in God. I found myself in a place that I couldn't recognize, and still I did not know who I was in Christ as his child. Once again trouble came in, but this time, I called on Jesus. Jesus came to my rescue, and he performed a miracle right before my eyes. Full of excitement, I thought to myself, *"The sun has begun to shine again in my life"*. I had to learn how to surrender and to submit to God's plan for my life. God had me in a place where I could no longer run from him. Instead, I welcomed God into my life after years of fighting him. I was finally ready to live my life for Christ without any regrets. I had imprisoned myself for years because I was running from my calling, but God used all my trials to change my character to look like his.

CHAPTER 1

How I Learned to Run Away

My life was about to change, and I was too young to fully understand what was about to happen. My dad was in the military, and it was my last year of school. My family and I were moving across the world to Japan. When I was told that we would have to move to Iwakuni, I was devastated. That meant that I would have to leave behind everything that I knew and loved, like my friends and my school.

When the time came for us to move away, I was so scared. This was something new for me, and I hated change. I became depressed quietly; my parents never knew how I was feeling on the inside. Everyone else in my family was excited about the move.

I was in pieces when we got on the plane. I had never been on an airplane before, and I didn't know what to expect. I asked to sit with my parents so I could hold their hands. The moment that plane landed in Iwakuni the place that would be our new home for the next two years, my thoughts were everywhere.

Struggling with My Emotions

I was hurting on the inside because I didn't want to have to start my life over. My dad tried to make the move easy for us. He even had our home set up for us; he had already been living in Japan for a year before we got there. I tried to like this new place. My dad even took us sightseeing. I wanted to enjoy this new adventure, but I was struggling with my emotions.

There were days that I would just sit in my room, crying and reminiscing about my old life. I had no one to talk with about my feelings, so I hid it from my parents. I tried to enjoy myself, but it felt like nothing was working for me. I even started writing to some people back in the States to help myself get through the rest of the summer. My Auntie Precious was one of those people.

After being in our new home for about a month, I was still crying every day—that is, until one day when I was sitting with my mom in our living room and everything went dark. My head was hurting so bad. I told my mom that I couldn't see anything, and she called the doctor. They made me an appointment that same day. Once we got there, the nurse asked me a lot of questions, and then the doctor came into the room and asked me even more questions so she could understand what was going on with me. She then checked me over and told my mom that I was depressed. The doctor spoke with my mom about keeping an eye on me because apparently the island that we were living on had a high rate of suicide. The doctor gave me some medicine to help with my headaches, which I had been getting just about every day since we had moved overseas.

When we got home, my mom spoke with me and said that I would feel better once I made some new friends. I did not want to make any friends, let alone stay there. So, for the rest of the summer, I just stayed at home and watched TV all day long.

Starting School

The time came for me to start school, and I didn't want to leave my house. I wanted to drop out of school and stay at home until it was time for us to leave for America. On the first day of school, my mom came into my room to give me some lunch money. I was crying on the floor. She asked me what was wrong, and I told her that I didn't want to go to school anymore. I said that I could get my GED, and then I could stay home.

My mom got really angry at me about that and told me that she washed her hands of me. She said that she didn't know what to do with me and left my room. My mom left my lunch money behind, though, hoping that I would change my mind. I became so emotional that I thought of taking my own life. It felt like I had no one that understood me. But God had a plan, because before my mom left my room that day, she gave me a letter that my auntie Precious had written to me.

I stood there with the same bottle of pills that the doctor had given me earlier in one hand and the letter in the other. Something was telling me to read the letter, so I opened it. Precious words saved my life that day. I had already been struggling with myself, and now on top of all that the enemy was telling me that my mom didn't want me anymore. I just cried as I read over her words again. Precious wrote that if anything ever happened to me, she wouldn't know what to do. See, God knew that this day would come, and he touched Precious's heart so that she would write me those words. In fact, he had to have touched her heart a week before that day, because I lived in Japan and she lived in the States. God not only had his hand on me but also knew that one day I would become his. I sat on the floor of my room crying because for the first time I felt like someone cared about me and how I really felt. I'd always felt like there was something missing in my life. Even as a young child, I struggled with being lonely. It took years for me to tell anyone about this day because I didn't want to get in trouble. Nor did I want anyone to judge me about it.

I started school the next day, but it wasn't easy for me because I just wanted my old friends and my life back. I was mad at my mom for a while because I didn't understand why she wouldn't let me just graduate with my friends. It took some time for me to get fully used to being in Japan. With time, I started making some friends, and I even started to date again. Still, my life overseas was a struggle, even after I met a lot of people and was starting to have fun. My school life was truly hard for me. I was always in trouble, and my grades were not the best. That part of my life I never got to enjoy because it felt like I didn't fit in with anyone. I was used to going to public school.

Finding Hope

Eventually I came around with school and began participating in different things there. I even joined the softball team and got to travel to different places around the area. I also started babysitting some of our friends' kids, just to keep myself busy. My friends and I started to explore the island by ourselves on the weekends. We would get on the local bus, which would take us around. We learned that bus schedule quickly. I started to find a group of friends that would make living here more exciting. I even took a class to get my driver's license so we didn't have to ride the bus anymore. That was a lot of fun. I learned a lot in that class, like how to change my own oil and fix my own tire.

Things were starting to look up for me, and this place was starting to grow on me finally. I'd never thought that I would be able to enjoy myself here, but my mom was right. I just needed to get connected with people my age. Then something that was once so dark to me became something so beautiful. Every day became an adventure with my new friends. I started to enjoy the culture around me. I was always gone on the weekends. But even though I was having fun, I still had a major issue: school. I was struggling with the teaching in every one of my classes.

I tried my hardest to get good grades, but there was a disconnect for me. I was used to the way teachers taught you in the States. God eventually placed a beautiful young teacher in my life, and she started helping and mentoring me. I went to her class every day just to talk and to get help with my lessons. This teacher became a good family friend of ours. I could talk to her about everything, and deep down that's what I needed in my life at that time. She kept me on the straight and narrow. She played no games with me and would break things down in a way that I could understand. That's what I needed—someone who would make time for me. She showed me that she really cared about me. I was able to understand my lessons from that point on.

Even though I now understood what was being taught to me, I still had to play makeup for all the months that I had fallen behind. I tried not to think about it too much because I didn't want to get back into that bad headspace again. I started to focus on just having fun. But in all truth, I was running away from my problems. I didn't know how to properly handle them and still be able to enjoy myself at the same time. I only knew how to focus on one thing at a time, and school was something I didn't want to focus on. I wanted to focus on making the good memories that I was now making. They became so powerful to me as I got older.

Learning to Embrace

I learned through this experience to never give up no matter how hard things look. There is always a greater meaning to everything if you will just stop and look for it. I did. I stopped making myself so sad and instead started to embrace this new journey that I was on. My tears turned into laughter every day. I was trying new things and learning how to embrace life, even if there were some challenges.

The food on the island of Iwakuni Japan was so amazing, and the people there were so nice. I learned a lot about the history of this new place, and I came to appreciate my life and everything that came with it. There were some things that I still never got used to, but I learned to accept things for what it was supposed to be.

Facing the Music

Time was moving by quickly for me, and I had to face the music. School was not going well at all. I had to study ten times harder than the other students just to get a passing grade on my exams. Because I'd chosen to run away from my one problem—my class assignments—I didn't know if I was even going to graduate high school at that moment. See, the enemy will never tell you what's on the other side of your wrong choices when you choose to listen to him. I wish I had just buckled down in the beginning. Now I was faced with the consequences. This where I wish I'd known God's word about the enemy. In John 10:10, Jesus tells us that "the thief cometh not, but for to steal, and to kill, and to destroy: I am come that they might have life, and that they might have it more abundantly."

Dealing with the consequences of my decisions was the hardest thing I had to do because now my parents were going to know the truth. I was messing up big time in school. There is one thing that I'd learned, which was that it is best to tell the truth in the beginning. So I did. I told my parents what was going on, and they helped me graduate high school.

The time was approaching when school would be over, but I didn't know what I wanted to do with my life. After graduation, my friends were headed back to the States for college. I, on the other hand, was headed to go live with my grandma Flo. I had a long talk with my parents about me leaving to go back to the States, and they were not happy about my decision to leave home so early.

Running Away

I had to leave for myself. My mom told me that I was making a big mistake, but she gave me her blessing. So I headed back to the States. Running away from my problems became one of my major issues as I got older. It would take me decades to be able to overcome that stronghold. You never know how one decision can change the whole course of your life.

Thinking I Knew It All

I was ready to live my life the way I wanted to; I was not going to let anyone tell me what to do again. I was nineteen years old. Facing the world for the first time, I thought that I knew it all, man. You couldn't tell me anything. When I got back to the States, I started hanging out every day and most of the nights. I would come into the house around about midnight or one o'clock in the morning. I didn't have a key, so I would have to wake up grandma Flo. This lifestyle went on for some months.

I was just happy to be free from the stressful life that I had been living in Iwakuni. I honestly never stopped to realize what I even wanted to do with my life. I had no goals. I didn't want to think about changing now; I was enjoying myself too much. I jumped in headfirst, and my only focus was me. The lessons that I had learned in Japan went right out of the window.

Learning about God

My grandma Flo, she would have long talks with me about God and how I needed to give my life to him. I would tell her that I was good with my life for now. I didn't know that grandma Flo was praying for me and that she was asking God to come into my life and change me. I would watch my grandma pray all the time; she would sing hymns throughout the day. I would ask her, "Why do you do all this?" My grandma Flo would always respond, "Keep living and you will see why I pray and sing to God."

She would get up early every morning and pray and sing to God as she cooked breakfast. She was showing me how to live a holy life before God daily; everything that she would do was centered around God.

Prayer Changing Experience

On one particular day, I was getting ready to walk out of my grandma's front door when grandma Flo and her friend started praying over me. It felt like something caught me in midair. Her friend put her hand on my forehead and began to pray. My auntie Bonnie was there too, and I remember falling into Bonnie's arms and just crying. Tears were running down my face, and I didn't know how to stop them.

My grandma and my auntie Bonnie were crying as well. The Spirit of God was moving in my grandma Flo's living room. I just cried as I heard my grandma's voice saying to me that God was going to save my life one day. See, I was not a bad kid, but I was not a good one either. My grandma Flo knew that I was fighting some major demons in my life.

7

My grandma Flo didn't just pray for me and walk away. She also called in the church for help. For the rest of the day, I just stayed close to home. I couldn't shake the feeling that no matter what I did, God had his hand on me. As I sit and write this book, I can't help but thank God for keeping me.

Showing Me the Way

My God had me in a place where I got to know my family and know that I still needed to be at home with my parents. I was not ready to be on my own yet, not like I thought I was. Things were changing in me. I no longer stayed out all night, and I started pulling back from talking to a lot of people. My grandma Flo was showing me how to become a disciple of Christ Jesus.

Going to Church

I spent six months living with my grandma Flo. The night of New Year's Eve 1999 my grandma took me and my cousins to church with her. I thought to myself that if the world was about to end, I wanted to be in the house of the Lord with my grandma Flo and my cousins. I was so happy to have gone to church that night because I was scared.

This moment brought back so many memories of my childhood. I remember that night on New Year's 1989, everyone was saying that the world was coming to an end. As a nine-year-old child, I was scared. But that night, my mom and her friends went to church and left all the kids at home.

When my mom left that night, I just stood in my front yard crying, looking up to the sky and asking God not to let me die by myself. That's why being with my grandma Flo that night at church was priceless. My grandma Flo always took time out for me during the period in my life that I stayed with her. No matter what she had, whether it was a lot or a little bit, she always made sure I witness her Christian lifestyle.

Telling Me the Truth

"My grandma always told me the truth" I love her for that. She was always telling me, "Girl you'd better sit down." My grandma Flo believed that God was going to change my life and that I would serve him and bring him glory. She never gave up on me and kept praying for me. I learned years later that she didn't want me to move back home with my parents. She said she'd wanted me to stay with her.

Going Back Home

After some time, my mom and my sisters sent for me to come back Iwakuni Japan. It was February of 2000. I was headed back to Iwakuni the same place that I'd run away from. I made that long trip back by myself. But something had changed inside me, and I didn't understand what it was.

God knew that this mindset of running was going to be a major problem in my life. I didn't recognize at the time that God was helping me to stop running, but I also didn't know to heed his voice at that time. I knew something had changed in my life. I fought against the change so I could get back to my old self again.

I got a job and started hanging out with older people, going to the club, and picking up bad habits. For months of my life, I had no one to pray over me like my grandma had, so I kept going to the club with my sister Coco, and Latrice and our friends. But after months of just trying to get "me" back, I found myself pulling away again from all that nightlife. My grandma Flo's prayers were working, because I didn't want to live like that anymore. She showed me how to want more out of myself.

Because I found myself wanting more, I decided to go into the military. I changed my lifestyle and started exercising and eating better, since I had gained so much weight since I got back home. I started feeling and looking better. Latrice joined me in my new lifestyle of exercising and eating healthier.

Moving with a Changed Mind

It was September of 2000, and it was time for my family to leave for the States. I was excited to be going into the military and to see my grandma Flo again. When I got back, grandma Flo was waiting for me. I loved being with my grandma Flo. Her love was everything to me.

Not Given Up

My grandma Flo told me the night before I went to take my test for the military that if I got to a place on the test that I didn't understand, I should recite Psalms 23. I didn't tell grandma Flo that I didn't know it. I just said yes ma'am and smiled as I got into the car to leave. That test was hard. I struggled with finishing my exam; all I could remember was grandma Flo's instruction to recite Psalms 23. I knew "The Lord is my Shepherd," but I was in trouble after that.

I made it through the rest of my test and headed back home, not knowing if I still wanted to go into the military or not. I knew I had to do something with my life, but I just didn't know what.

No Direction in Life

I decided to leave grandma Flo's house to go back and stay with my parents so I could regroup and figure out what I wanted to do with myself. My sister Coco and I were the only ones who still lived at home, but Coco was getting ready to get married and move away soon.

All I did was sit in the house with my sister Coco and my nephews Alexander, and Marquis watching time go by. I had lost all my focus in life. I had a lot of things that I needed to change about myself; I just didn't know where to start. There were days that I would just write. Writing gave me peace because everything would get so quiet and still during that time.

Eventually my sister Coco got married and it came time for her and my nephew Marquis to leave home to start their new life. When she left, I went to stay with my sister Latrice for about two weeks. In that two weeks, God changed my life forever.

> The Lord is my shepherd; I shall not want. He maketh me lie down in green pastures: He leadeth me beside the still waters. He restoreth my soul; He leadeth me in the paths of righteousness for his name sake. Yea, though I walk through the valley of the shadow of death, I will fear no evil: for thou art with me: thy rod and thy staff they comfort me. Thou prepared a table before me in presence of mine enemies: thou anointest my head with oil my cup runneth over. Surely goodness and mercy shall follow me all the days of my life: and I will dwell in the house of the Lord for ever. (Psalms 23)

This was the very first scripture that I learned. I wanted to know it for myself. I read that verse over and over until I knew it by heart. I wanted to change my life. I knew that I was hurting, and I was tired of the way I was living. I knew there was something more for me. I just didn't know how to get it. I was not going to give up, though.

CHAPTER 2

Coming to Christ

I arrived at my sister Latrice and her boyfriend's Wayne apartment. I was in this place in my life in which I was longing for something. I felt this pulling on my heart all the time. I didn't say anything to Latrice about it because I didn't know what it was. Latrice told me that they had started going to church. I went with them the whole time that I was there. I started feeling like something was missing in my life, though I couldn't put my finger on it. But I kept going to church with them every Sunday.

On one particular Sunday morning, I was sitting in church, and it seemed like the pastor was speaking just to me and me alone. I felt something inside of me telling me to give my life to God, and I was ready.

My sister's boyfriend Wayne at the time looked at me and said, "The pastor is talking about you."

I said, "I know."

Giving My Life to Christ

Wayne asked me if I wanted him to go with me into the room for prayer, and I said yes because I didn't want to be alone. I went into the room and saw that there were a lot of people giving their lives to Christ. The ministers came over to me and asked me if I was ready to give my life to Christ. I said yes. The ministers started praying over me, and again the tears started falling down. I lifted up my hands before God and accepted Christ into my life that Sunday morning. As we left church that day, I was thanking God for coming into my life.

I called my grandma Flo and told her that I had given my life to Christ. I could hear the excitement in her voice over the phone. She was praising God! My grandma said, "What did I tell you? That God was going to save your life." We were both so excited about God's plan for me.

I knew that I would have to go back home, but deep down inside I didn't want to go. I wanted to stay with Latrice and Wayne so I could keep going to church with them. I didn't want to think about that, so I just enjoyed the time I had left with them. I felt so light, and my mind was relaxed and full of peace. I eventually returned to my parent's house not knowing if I was still going to be able to go to church, but God had a plan.

My new life was beginning, and I started reading my Bible and praying. One day a friend came over, and we got to talking. I asked her if I could go to church with her, and she said yes. For several months she would come and pick me up to take me to church. She took me under her wing, and I started growing in Christ. God started moving in my life like never before. I was now living a life that I was proud of. I got a job not too far from my home and started going to church on a regular basis. I was no longer searching for anything. I was in the best place in my life, even though I was still at home with my parents. I was OK with that. I started taking some college classes online.

God Making a Way

After some time, my friend told me that she wasn't going to be able to pick me up for church anymore. I told her that was fine because I had gotten my first paycheck and had asked my dad if he could go with me to look for a car. He took me that weekend, and I bought my first car. God did not allow me not to have a way to church.

I was learning just who God really was in my life. God cared so much about me. I had been looking for someone all my life to love me like this. God's love is unexplainable; it's just amazing.

Sharing My Faith

At this point I started sharing my faith with everyone. I told everyone about God. I still remember the day God led me to this passage in 1 Corinthians:

> Love is patient, love is kind. It does not envy, it does not boast, it is not proud. It does not dishonor others, it is not self-seeking, it is not easily angered, it keeps no record of wrongs. Love does not delight in evil but rejoices with the truth. It always protects, always trusts, always hope, always preserves. (1 Corinthians 13:4–7 NIV)

After I read this verse, I was filled with so much love. I immediately ran into my mom's room to share this verse with her. This verse became my favorite for years of my life. I tried my hardest to live by it. I became a woman who gave so much love to other people. I did not want to be mad at anyone; I just wanted to love like God was telling me to. I helped my parents with my little nephew Alexander, who they were raising. I poured all my love into him because he and I were the only ones living with my parents at the time.

New Outlook

I started meeting new people at work. Sometimes I would hang out with one of the girls on the weekend. Still, I didn't let the people in my life get in the way of my relationship with Jesus; I was too in love with Christ. I would only talk about Christ with them. I continued to make time for Christ, and I worshipped every day just, like grandma Flo had shown me.

Vision through Dreams

God started showing me dreams. Some of them I couldn't understand, and I would call my grandma Flo so she could help me understand them better. I knew that God had called me to be a prayer warrior, and I had started praying for my family. I remember the first dream that God showed me. In it, my dad's mom, my grandmother, passed away. When I woke up from that dream, I called grandma Flo, my mom's mom, who I had stayed with for a short time. I told her about some of my dream but not all of it. She told me to go to prayer. Grandma Flo told me to ask God to give me understanding of what he was showing me. I said, "Yes, ma'am."

When I got off of the phone, I did just what she had told me. I asked God for understanding. I then left and went to church. When I got back home, my mom came to the door and told me that my grandmother had died. That was the hardest day of my life. I punched the wall in our hallway and fell to my knees crying. I thought it was my fault because I had prayed for understanding.

I ran into my room to call grandma Flo and tell her the rest of my dream because I had left out a major part. I'd left out the part where my mom and I were walking through some apartments and a little boy came up to me and told me that it's nice in heaven. I thought that if I told her the rest of my dream that would make my dad's mom come back to us. That was not true at all; she was still gone. I never got to say goodbye to her before she passed away.

Struggling with My Faith

Being so young with a gift like this and not having anyone to guide me in that gift was really hard for me. I didn't fully understand my gift of visions. I'd never had anyone talk to me about the different gifts that God gave to his children. I allowed my fears to stop me from praying for people. I thought that my prayers were hurting people instead of helping them. I did not understand God's will for other people's life. My grandmother's death really did something to me spiritually.

When I saw my grandmother for the last time at her funeral to say goodbye, I broke down and fell to the ground crying. Afterward I sat outside in my dad's truck by myself, just worshipping God with gospel music. I was listening to Sam Cooke's "Peace in the Valley." I cried out to God for help because I was struggling with my emotions that day.

I learned very early in life to just pull back from people when I am going through something. That's what I started to do after my grandmother's funeral. When some of my family members would talk to Mom on the phone, they would tell her to ask me to pray for them. But I would say no thanks. My mom told me that I was supposed to pray and that God wanted me to pray for others, but I thought that my gift was a curse and struggled with it. So, I went on with my life and went back to work. Even though I was hurting, however, I never stopped believing in God. I kept going to church and kept reading my Bible.

I became content with my new routine: work, church, and college in that order. I never had anyone to talk to about my gifts. I was told that when you got saved you had to join a church, and that was it, I thought. I wanted to serve Christ; I knew that God had come into my life. I just wasn't mature enough in Christ at that time. I was still a new babe in Christ. I wanted someone to mentor me, but I didn't know who. I was basically learning on my own to be a Christian the best way I knew how. I didn't know that God was taking me through a process—the process of dying to my flesh and surrendering my will to his will. I was still struggling with my faith at this time. I became a person for whom just going to church on Sunday morning was enough.

My Mom Coming to Church

Even though I was content with just going to church only on Sunday mornings, God was still using me. My mom started going to church with me, and we both joined the church and started the process to get baptized. We got close to finishing the required class when my mom had to stop going to church in order to do her job. She now had to work on Sundays. I kept going to the class and got baptized in November 2001.

Meeting My Friend

Shortly after my baptism, I met this amazing young woman who worked with me. Tasha became a good friend. She was a Christian as well, and she welcomed me into her family. Tasha modeled for me what a Christian wife and mother should look like. Even though I was not married and did not have kids at that time, God knew that I was going to need this woman and her family in my life. Tasha is an amazing woman of God. I watched her as she served him. We didn't go to the same church, but we both shared the same love for Jesus.

Tasha became my only friend. She would pray for me, and there were days that she would tell me things that God had shown her about me. I had run away from my gift in Christ before she came into my life, but Tasha showed me that it was a blessing for God to use you to help someone else. Having someone in my life who had one of the same gifts as I did in Jesus gave me hope. I admired the person she was. Our families became really close after that, and I started hanging out more at her house. Her home was always so peaceful to me. I wanted something like that when I got married too.

After a while, I started longing for something more, like marriage and kids. I started to crave a husband, but not just any husband. I wanted a husband who would pray with me and go to church with me as well. If I'd known then what I know now, I would have waited to find a husband until God had removed all of me out of me.

Learning There Is More

I was saved but not delivered yet at this time. See, there is a major difference between the two. I had a lot of healing and growing to do. On one particular Sunday, I visited Tasha's church. I went up for prayer, and the first lady of the church prayed for me. She whispered in my ear, telling me that God was going to give me a husband but that I had to stop looking. She said, "You're not looking in your feet, but you are looking in your mind." I understood what she was saying to me even though I was not going out looking for a husband I was always thinking about finding my husband. As I would go throughout my day, I would see young men crossing my path, and the first thing I would think was, *Could that be my husband?*

Praying for a Husband

After church that day, I came home and prayed to God. Then I stopped—I stopped wondering who was going to be my husband. I even tore up the letter I had written to God about the kind of husband that I desired. I started to believe that whatever and whoever God had for me, he would give it to me at the right time. Sometimes we can run ahead of God, especially when we already know that God is going to give something to us. Though my husband now is the man that God gave me, I wish I had trusted God's timing.

Maybe a month after the first lady spoke to me, my mom came into my room and told me that she'd had a dream. God had shown her my husband. My mom went on to describe this guy. She told me that God told her that this man was going to treat me so well. I really couldn't believe that because of my past relationship. I laughed at her and I said, "That can't be real." She told me to watch and see. After that day I didn't think too much about her dream.

How I Met My Husband

One day one of my old friends reached out to me by email; back then people were not texting. He wrote to me and sent me pictures of his journey in Japan. Before I go into deeper detail, though, let me take you back to two years before.

On May 19, 2000, I was living in Japan with my parents. On this particular day, my dad had to have surgery, so my parents asked me to drive them to the airport. I did. But what I didn't know was that God was going to show me my husband. As I walked into the terminal at the airport, I looked to my right, and there was this handsome guy. He was in the military, and he had the sleeves of his uniform rolled up. All I saw was his tattoos. I was moved by them. I wanted a bad-boy kind of guy in my life, and I thought that this guy could be him. But no, this guy was far from a bad boy. I would soon find out that he was a Christian.

I went to his Staff Sergeant and asked him who that guy was, and he told me his name. I told the Staff Sergeant that I wanted to meet him, and he politely said, "No. He is a good person, and I do not want you to corrupt him." I told him that I wouldn't do that; I just wanted to meet him.

So later on that evening, the young man walked to my house. Everyone was standing outside in the parking lot of our home. I saw this guy from a distance walking down the hill toward the sidewalk. His Staff Sergeant lived across the street from us at the time, and I looked at him and asked him if it was this was the guy from before. He answered yes. I told the Staff Sergeant that I didn't want to meet this guy anymore. I had a change of heart at that moment; the guy looked different out of uniform. But the young man proceeded to come to the house anyway. We met and exchanged names. I thought that he was too nice for me and that we could just be friends.

We all started talking, and a group of us thought it would be a good idea to go to a local mom-and-pop shop in the area. It was a great outing. I got to talk more with the young man and get to know him a little better. It was Mother's Day weekend, so we all bought something there for our moms. The guy and I just talked as friends. I knew that I would be moving soon, so I didn't want to date him. He had plans to stay another year in Japan. So we left everything on a friendship level.

How We Stayed Connected

Now, when September was upon us and it was time for my family to move back to America, this young man was invited to my sister Coco's going away party. He worked with her at his second job. The party was amazing. I sat across from the young man all night. It was the first time he had seen me after I lost all my weight, and I believe that it was the first time that he took notice of me as well. After we left the restaurant where the party had been held, we went to a little nightclub. This young man began to sing, and I was blown away by his voice. It was so powerful. I wanted him to sing to me all night. As the night came to an end, the young man asked me if I could give him a ride home. When I dropped him off at his room, he asked me for my information. He wanted us to stay in touch, and we did.

We stayed friends over the years. When he came back from Japan, he came to visit me and my family for the weekend. I told him that he would be my best friend, so if I had any guy problems I could come and talk with him. He told me that it would be fine for me to call on him. I never actually called him about guys, though. If I'd only known God's plan back then, it would have saved me a lot of bad relationships.

He went back home, and we didn't speak for a while after that weekend—not until the day he started emailing me out of the blue. I didn't think anything of it until the emails started to come more often.

My Mom's Dreams Were Real

I started to like this man; his words were always the right words at the right time. I began to get antsy waiting for his emails to come. I wrote to him to ask him for his phone number. He gave it to me that night, and I couldn't wait to talk with him. It was a Thursday evening. The young man did not live near me, so I had to wait until he got off work in his time zone. Let me tell you, those hours of waiting till I could call him were long. So as soon as the time came that I could call him, I did. When he answered the phone, I could hear in his voice that he was sick. I asked him if he was getting sick and said that if he was, he should take some medicine. He said that he was going to, but first he had to clean up his room for his inspection. So, we got off the phone.

After that evening, we spent hours on the phone just talking. It was mainly just me talking; he was a good listener. I'd finally found a man that would talk to me about God and would pray for me. I'd thought this could only happen in the movies. I told him that I'd given my life to Christ and that I had gotten baptized, and he was so happy for me. He would send me scriptures to read for encouragement.

I was falling in love with him quickly. I called my sister Coco I told her that I wanted to date this guy. Coco and I called him on three way when he answered the phone Coco said to him that Colandra likes you and want to date you. He responded with yes, only because it's Colandra, him didn't believe in long distance relationships. We started dating in March. We both decided that I would come and visit him, so I did. After I got back home from my trip, he told me that he was going to go on vacation to see his family. He asked me if I wanted to come with him so I could meet them, and I said yes.

Meeting His Family

He gave me the dates that he was taking vacation so I could take the same dates off as well. I asked my mom if she wanted to take a road trip with me, since Latrice my sister lived in his hometown. My mom said yes, since Latrice had just had her first baby and she could go see them. When the day came for us to leave, I was so excited to see this man again. He was so special to me. He treated me with so much respect.

The day after we arrived, he took me to meet his family, and my breath was taken away by the way he cared for me. He made me feel so special that whole trip. One day, after that trip was over and I had headed back home, we started talking over the phone about getting married. I didn't think that we would be getting married so quickly. It was just us talking, I told myself, but I really wanted to spend the rest of my life with him. He had become my best friend, and I trusted him with my whole heart.

The Engagement

One day over the phone he asked me to marry him. I was so excited. I did not hesitate to say yes either. I couldn't wait to be with him for the rest of my life. We both called his mom to tell her the good news, and she said, "I knew this was going to happen." She said that he'd never brought a girl to their house to meet them.

I told my parents that I was getting married, and mom smiled because I hadn't believed her dream. Now everything that God had shown her was coming to pass. God had already known that back when I returned back to my parents' home in Japan. He had allowed my husband and I to meet then because he had a plan for us.

My good friend gave me a card with a scripture in it once, and it changed my world. It was from Matthew 7:7–8: "Ask, and it shall be given you; seek, and ye shall find; knock, and it shall be opened unto you: for every one that asketh receiveth; and he that seeketh findeth; and to him that knocketh it shall be opened." Whenever I get into a place of "I don't know," I remember these verses.

God reminds us in Matthew 6:6–8, "But thou, when thou prayest, enter into thy closet, and when thou hast shut thy door, pray to thy Father which is in secret; and thy Father which seeth in secret shall reward thee openly. But when ye pray, use not vain repetitions, as the heathen do: for they think that they shall be heard for their much speaking. Be not ye therefore like unto the: for your Father knoweth what things ye ask him." These teachings help me to understand God's plans for my life and how he has given me dominion over my prayers.

CHAPTER 3

Fighting for Our Home

In September 2002, my husband and I got married, and I moved in with him. We drove across the country and honeymooned at the same time. It was a beautiful moment but at the same time a scary moment. I was now someone's wife. My husband told me that he expected me to help him drive during the three-day trip. My brother John even told my husband that I didn't drive long distances. I responded with yes, I do. I didn't believe I had a real issue with driving, but I did. He said that he was going to get our marriage annulled within that first day because I didn't drive. We each had some expectations about the other. He thought that I could drive long distances. I thought that a man should never let a woman drive if he was in the car with her. That's what my dad taught us; my mom never had to drive if my dad was with her. I expected that as well. God blessed us to be able to make it to our new home, where we would live for the next three years, but that drive showed us that we both had a lot of expectations to let go of.

A month after living together, I started to see some traits in myself that I had previously either watched or just suppressed entirely. I started to see that I was very needy of my husband's attention. I wanted to be with him all the time. I thought that's what husbands and wives were supposed to do. I realize now that I was trying to

23

mimic my friend's marriage because in my eyes it was so peaceful and beautiful at the same time. But I was skipping the whole process of getting to know one another. I just wanted to jump into this perfect picture of what I thought marriage should look like.

My expectations of marriage were not the same as my husband's. Still, we were so in love that we overlooked that issue we were facing. We just made everything work the best way we knew how so we could get past it quickly.

New Roles in Life

Two months after saying I do, we learned that we were going to have a baby. We were so excited. I thought that I was the luckiest woman in the world to be having my husband's baby. I was only twenty-two years old, and my pregnancy brought me all kinds of emotions. I was soon going to find out what kind of mom I was going to be. I did not know half of what I thought I knew about being pregnant and becoming a mom.

Learning about Me

I was about four months pregnant when the doctor gave me my first ultrasound. I was so excited. But as the doctor looked at the screen, she saw that I had 100 percent placenta previa. My husband and I did not know what that meant. The doctor said that I would have to have a C-section when the time came for me to have our baby. She explained what that meant and said it was going to be a very closely monitored pregnancy. She told me that I was restricted from heavy lifting and that mine was a high-risk pregnancy.

I was scared at that time because I had this perfect picture in my head of what my life was going to look like. What I didn't know was that God was allowing me to go through this for a reason. Fifteen years later, I would find myself encouraging a young lady who was facing the same thing that I had. God never allows you to go through something hard for nothing.

My husband and I started praying and trusting in God. We joined an amazing church, and we had an amazing support group in our church family. They adopted us as their children, and we knew then that things were going to be fine. We had so many people that encouraged us and prayed for us. Our marriage and our pregnancy were dreams come true to me. No matter what we were facing, we had each other, and that's all that I needed.

Prayers

When time came for me to have my C-section, our pastor met us at the hospital at 6:30 a.m. It was the best feeling in the world to have my husband and pastor Don at my side. When the nurses came into my room to get me for the C-section, our pastor said to them, "Before you take her back, would you give me a moment to pray with the family." Some of the nurses smiled at us because as first-time soon-to-be parents we had brought our pastor with us.

I thought to myself, *What a mighty God we serve. To be able to have all this love and support in the room with me.* Our daughter was born, and now life began. My doctor was amazing. My C-section went very well, from the beginning to the end. I knew that God was with me through it all.

New beginnings

God had his hands on my whole pregnancy, but when we got home, it was just me and my husband with this little tiny six-pound baby girl. The tears started to come down the moment I laid my eyes on my baby. I started to praise God because he had given me everything that I had been praying for. I had my husband and our baby. I was blessed. That moment was also when so many fears came into my heart. I wanted to be a good mom for this little girl. I cried until I just said to God, "Please help me to be the best mom I can be for her."

But some months later on, my flesh took over. See, this is the part of my life that I would not have had to go through if I had gone through the process of surrendering my fears to God in the beginning of my Christian walk. My mind wouldn't allow me to enjoy every part of my new blessing. I was trapped with a stronghold in my mind. I thought that I had to help God with everything when it came to taking care of my daughter. I was so scared that I was becoming very overprotective with my daughter. Fear had a major grip on me to the point that I couldn't recognize myself anymore as a child of God, as a wife, or as a mother. I was robbing my husband of his bonding experience with our daughter because I didn't trust anybody but myself. I wanted to trust everyone, but I thought I had to do it all by myself. I was her mom, and I believed that she only needed me. I was a young first-time mom who was scared, and I didn't want anyone to know that I was scared. I just wanted everything to look like my dreams and to follow the plan that I had for myself as a wife and a mother. Everyone I knew made being a mom look so easy, but I made it so hard. I told my husband that I was going to talk with my doctor on my next visit.

During my checkup with my doctor, I spoke with her about how I had been feeling most days since my daughter was born. She told me some signs to watch out for, because she didn't want me to go through postpartum depression. She told me that some women after pregnancy will experience this. I had already gone through depression as a teenager. I didn't want to feel that way as a wife and mother. One day I cried out to God for help. I didn't like who I was becoming. I spoke with my husband about everything that I was feeling. I told him that I was going to have the pastor Don pray for me at church on Sunday morning.

When church was over that day, my husband and I went and spoke with our pastor, and he began to pray over our family. The pastor spoke life into me that day, and I felt so much better. I knew that I had to stay before God if I wanted to be healthy. My prayer life increased. I prayed about everything in my life. There was a calmness that came to me when I would worship God. I started singing to God every day, and that uncertainty began to turn around. Where there once was fear of raising my daughter, now there was pure determination.

My daughter gave me a reason to fight to change my life for the better, even when it came to driving. I spent a year not really driving too far away from home until one day when my daughter was in need of her new medicine and my husband was not available to pick it up for me. I prayed and asked God to take my fear of driving away from me. I was determined to get my daughter's medicine. God answered me right away. I got in that car and drove by myself with my daughter, and I have been driving my car without fear ever since then. I believe in the power of prayer. Philippians 4:6 says, "Be careful for nothing, but in everything by prayer and supplication, with thanksgiving, let your requests be made known to God; and the peace of God, which surpasses all understanding, shall keep your hearts and minds through Christ Jesus."

My joy in being a wife and a mom depended on me not worrying about whether I was making a mistake. I had to tell myself that if I made a mistake along the way, it would be alright. I had to let myself off the hook. I was not perfect, and things were going to be messy at times. But the important thing was going to be how I handled those messy moments. Yes, I was still overprotective with my daughter—that was going to take some time—but my family and I started having fun together. Our daughter became the highlight of our home her smile brought so much peace into any room.

My daughter was what my husband and I needed. I watched God start to change things in our lives. My husband started singing in the choir at our church. He was giving up his life for God. It was beautiful to watch him serve God through music. Even if my daughter and I were visiting family, my husband still went to church. We made sure that God was first in our home.

My husband came home one day with news; we would be moving closer to our families. We were excited to be able to be a part of special events with our family that till now we hadn't been able to be a part of. Still, as the time came closer for us to move, it became harder to leave our church family. They had become a big part of our family journey. My dad flew in to help us drive across the country. This drive was not bad at all. We moved at the same time our daughter was being potty trained. I had to think outside of the box with this one.

I brought her potty chair with us in the car. It sat in the back of our car on the floor. If she had to go, she was still able to go whenever she needed to. I did not want to mess up her training. It turned out to be an amazing thing. We had no issues with it at all.

The New Move

We made it to our new location in North Carolina. We even got to spend time with family, some of whom were getting to meet our daughter for the first time. It was an amazing feeling watching her play with her cousins and try new things. We got the keys to our new home, where we would spend the next three years. It was different going from a one-bedroom apartment to a three-bedroom townhouse. We were there for about a month before we found our new church home. One thing my husband and I talked about before marriage was sharing of faith in Christ with each other. My husband was brought up in church; my family, not so much. I wanted that to be different, so we made it our business to stay active in church no matter where we moved.

Things were now moving along in my life for the good. Our daughter turned two years old, and my husband and I talked about me going to work and putting our daughter into daycare for the first time in her life. I was so excited for the new change in our lives.

There are things that you forget along the way when you are happy, like the fact that when children enter daycare for the first, their little bodies have to become immune to the new viruses and other sicknesses. You all know what comes with a sick child? Missing days from work so you can take care of your sick child. That was an adjustment for us, having our baby get sick her first month of being in daycare. It was not easy. We did our best to make things work. My husband and I split up the days that one of us would have to stay home as she recovered. My job was not as understanding as my husband's job was. He was able to take time off. I would have to get up early so I could call off of work. That was not fun, especially since I had only been on the job for about a month. My husband and I talked about what would be best for our family. We knew that I still needed to work; the best thing was for me to work from home. So that's what I started doing. It was the best decision. There was one problem, however: the more I stayed home, the readier I was to have another baby.

Praying with Faith

I spoke with my husband about us having another baby, and his answer was "not now." But I thought that this would be the best time in our lives to have more kids. I had become a woman who truly believed in prayer, so I started talking with God about this. It was on a Sunday morning after church that I decided to bring this issue back up with my husband. Once again, his answer was "I am not ready to have any more kids." He said that he was not saying no to having more kids, but he was not saying yes either.

I felt like that talk got us nowhere, and I really wanted to have a son. I came from a large family, and my plan for my life had always been to have three children. I didn't want our daughter to be alone. There were days that my husband would talk about baby names. One day he said to me, "This would be a nice name for our baby." In my head I figured he was ready. I decided to seek God's face through fasting and prayer. I cried out to God to show me his plan for my family, and I trusted that he would. I left it in his hands.

Within a month of me praying, God favored me once again. I was pregnant, but I didn't know it yet—not until one day at church when I stood next to this woman and she looked at me. I told her good morning, and with her next breath she told me I was pregnant. I told her, "No, ma'am. I am not." I didn't know what to think the whole time I was in church.

I told my husband what this woman had told me, and he asked me, "Well, are you?"

I told him, "No. Why would you ask me that?"

He said, "Because you haven't asked for your favorite cookies."

I hadn't thought about it. I didn't have a craving for them like I usually did every month. I decided to get a test from the store one

Saturday morning while I was shopping. When I got home, I found to my surprise that we were indeed pregnant. I was over the moon about God's plan for my family. On the other hand, when I told my husband the news, he was not excited.

I didn't know what to do. My husband was struggling with us having another baby. On the outside everything looked great in our home, but on the inside, there was so much resentment. While I had been praying secretly for a baby, my husband had been making plans to get out of the military. Even though I had spoken with my husband about my feelings on having more kids, he'd never spoken with me about his plans. We were now on two different pages in our home. This was not good.

A Quiet Home

The enemy came in fast, and my husband was starting to become very quiet with me. He is already a quiet person, but this was a different kind of quiet. Our once so happy life gave way to a quite lonely home. I cried for most of the beginning of my pregnancy. God knew I needed some words of encouragement. One day out of the blue, my husband's granny called me. She said to me, "God doesn't want you to be sad at his blessings." She started praying against miscarriages. I didn't know why, because to my knowledge everything was fine. God had showed her what I couldn't see. She told me to stop all that crying and start rejoicing. As we got off the phone, I thanked her for encouraging me, because I didn't know what to do. After the call, my mom called me and talked to me about the same thing. God saw the secret cry inside of my heart.

I started trusting God, and I allowed myself to be happy again. I had thought that if my husband was sad, I had to be as well. God was saying, *No, I will turn this around what Satan means for evil and turn it to good.* God had a bigger plan that would be revealed to us later on. We had to learn to trust blindly at times, just like in Hebrews 11:1: "Now faith is the substance of things hoped for, the evidence of things not seen." Even though we couldn't see that God was working on behind the sense, he really was working everything out for us.

We found out that we were having a boy, and I was over the moon about it. I'd always wanted a little boy. Our daughter was so happy that she was going to be a big sister. I even took her with me to my doctor's appointments so that she could feel like she was a part of the pregnancy as well. After some time went by, my husband started to come around to having a son. I stayed in prayer with God and put all my trust in him during this season in our life. Now, this pregnancy was not high risk like my last pregnancy with my daughter.

As the time came for me to give birth to our son, I started to become nervous. I knew there was going to be some recovery time. I didn't know how I was going to recover with a four-year-old at home. We made arrangements for my mom to get our daughter for us. That was a major blessing.

The night before my C-section, we tried to eat dinner, but all we could do was pray. My husband and I prayed that God would watch over me and our son.

God Was Working Things Out

We were in our hospital room after having our son that morning when God did something amazing. My husband held our son in his arms, and when he looked into our son's eyes, he told him, "I am sorry." I thought to myself, *Look at God*. This was the most beautiful moment I had ever witnessed between a father and his son. When we got home, it was nice having my husband step up and take over with our son.

I just knew the enemy was no longer hurting my family. One weeks after our son's birth, our daughter came home so she could meet her baby brother. I noticed my husband starting to become uneasy around the house. I didn't understand what was going on with him; I thought he was happy. In reality, the enemy had a grip on his heart, but God was still working things out for us. I never gave up on prayer. I knew God's word, and I stood on his word. I blamed myself for my husband's sadness. I told myself that if I just would have waited for my husband to say yes, everything would have been fine. I carried that feeling for years until God delivered me from it all.

During all this time, my husband was not going to church because he had to work on the weekends. That's why the enemy was able to play with his mind, I believe. But God had a bigger plan; the whole time he was working on everyone's heart. God's plan was not just for my husband to go to church; it was to bring my husband back to him. Within a month after our son was born, God opened a major door.

My husband was able to change jobs, and we could go to church together again as a family. Our pastor once preached on Isaiah 43:2: "When thou passest through the waters, I will be with thee; and through the rivers, they shall not overflow thee: When thou walkest through the fire, thou shalt not be burned; neither shall the flame kindle upon thee." These words were so true. God had his hands on my family. I can't stop thanking him enough. Hearing these words taught that day at church gave me so much hope for our future. No matter what it is that you are facing in life, make God bigger than the problem.

God tells us in John 15:16, "Ye have not chosen me, but I have chosen you, and ordained you, that ye should go and bring forth fruit, and that your fruit should remain: that whatsoever ye shall ask of the Father in my name, he may give it you." I asked God to give me back my family, our peace, our joy, and our home. God chose us before we were even born; he knew that we would be his children. As we got back to our routine of praying and going to church, our home was home again.

This was just the beginning of the work we still had to do in our marriage, however. The battle was not won just yet. In the years ahead, God would teach us how to love one another. He would teach us how to be husband and wife. We still had a lot of growing pains to go through before we could be who God had called us to be for each other. Throughout our journey, God would place a lot of husbands and wives in our lives to serve as models. When I prayed for God to give me back my family, God didn't stop until everything was restored.

The time came for us to move again, but this time we would have to fight. Our lives were changed forever with this move. God was with us through it all.

> But ye are a chosen generation, a royal priesthood, an holy nation, a peculiar people; that called ye should shew forth the praises of him who called you out of darkness into his marvellous light. (1 Peter 2:9)

CHAPTER 4

Best Days Turned into Darkness

The time had come for us to move away from my parents. We were not happy about this move, but we had to trust God. We immediately started to get settled into our new home. After a day of being there, we started to find our way around. This was nothing new for us; moving was a part of our life. Our children were still young at this time. I told myself that this move would be different. I was on fire for Jesus, and I was studying his word daily. So I started to trust in God's plan for this new move.

Our furniture had not yet arrived to our new home, so we had to sleep on an air mattress until the movers came. One day I noticed a bump on the back of my leg. I asked my husband to look at it, and he started touching my leg. I started yelling for him to stop touching me. He told me that he was not even touching the bump and said I should go to the doctor to get my leg checked out.

Fearing without Praying

I made an appointment that day, and the doctor was able to see me that evening. When she came into the room, she looked at my leg and asked me if I knew what MRSA was. I said, "Yes. Why?" She told me she thought I had it. She had to run some tests on the fluid that was in my leg to determine if it was MRSA or not, so she made a little incision where the bump was. When she was done, she applied some medicine to the area and covered the area with a bandage. The doctor then gave me some instructions on how to care for my leg during this healing time. Afterward I called my dad crying to tell him about what the doctor had said. He gave me some words of encouragement. I was scared because I didn't know what the outcome of this would be.

I went to pick up my medicine, and when I got back home, I told my husband what was going on. At that point, fear gripped me again. My husband kept telling me that God had not brought us this far to leave us. He said, "Babe, you will be OK." I heard him, but my mind was thinking about my kids and how I wanted to be able to take care of them. I didn't know how to count it all joy, as the Bible tells us to do in James 1:2—"My brethren, count it all joy when ye fall into divers temptations." I wouldn't allow myself to receive my husband's words of strength. I was scared that I was going to die and that my kids were going to be without me.

I had to wait about a week before I got my test results back. I cried so many days and prayed every day during my wait. One day my husband sat me down. He told me that he had been watching me for days just crying. He said to me, "You are going to live; you are not going to die. So, stop acting like you are. Don't you have faith in God? Your test will be fine. Babe, I don't believe that you even have what the doctor said." Afterward my husband had to leave the house for a couple of hours. While he was gone, I watched my kids playing in the living room and started to cry.

My Hope Being Restored

I asked God to spare my life and said that I would follow him and find a church to be a part of. By this time my husband had made it back home. I called our pastor Jay from our last church home in North Carolina. I wanted him to pray with my family about the outcome of my situation. Pastor Jay told my husband to get some olive oil and go into a room alone and pray over it. He also told my husband to anoint the foreheads of everyone in our home with the oil and to pray over our family that God will cover us.

My husband got the family in a circle in the middle of our living room floor and began to pray like never before. I felt my strength returning to me, and I stopped feeling sorry for myself and started praising God for everything that he was doing for my family.

I talked with my mom, and she said that God had always given me everything that I wanted. She said, "You'd better stop acting like God is not good. You'd better get up and stop all that crying and know that God is going to make it alright." I smiled, said yes ma'am, and then stopped worrying about my test results and started living my life again.

Monday came, and the doctor called me to tell me that I did not have MRSA, that it was just an infection from a spider bite. I knew at that point that the spider had bitten me when I laid on that air mattress that night. The doctor told me to stop taking the medicine for MRSA and instead put me on some new medicine. I told her thank you and went to pick up my new medicine so I could start it that day.

Right after I got off of the phone, I started praising God like never before. I just held my family in my arms, smiling. God is so good! We were so happy after that call.

"See, babe, I told you that you were going to be OK," my husband said, smiling at me with his pretty brown eyes.

A Turnaround in My Faith

From that day forward, I was focused on God's plan for my life. We joined a local church, and I started to serve God like never before. One day when my kids were taking a nap, I went into my bedroom and cried out to God to come into my life and forgive me for all my sins. God's word tells us in Romans 6:22, "But now being made free from sin, and becoming servants to God, ye have your fruit unto holiness, and the end everlasting life."

I wanted God to change me for his plan. God started moving quickly in my life after that prayer of repentance. I started teaching at our church and sharing my testimony with people because I knew that God had come into my life and changed my mindset. I wanted everyone to feel like I was feeling. I didn't want anyone to have to be broken. I couldn't stop smiling because of God. I was made new, and I was walking into my newness. It felt so good.

> Therefore, if any man be in Christ, he is a new creature: old things are passed away; behold, all things are become new. (2 Corinthians 5:17)

That's how my life had begun to feel: new again. My family started to see the change that God had done in my life. They knew that God had called me to be a prayer warrior earlier in my life, and they started calling me so I could pray for them. Even our pastor Jay from back home would call me to pray for some of the members at the church.

God was moving so mightily in my life. I wanted to share my joy with everyone that I came in contact with. I wanted to share my new life with grandma Flo, so I called grandma Flo and asked her if she wanted to take a free vacation to my house. She said yes. I bought her first plane ticket, and she got on a plane for the first time. I was so excited to have her in our home. We did everything together. She started going to church with my family. I was excited for my grandma to be going to church with me now. She'd once prayed that God would save me. Now she got to see for herself her prayers being answered. Her eyes would light up when I would talk with her about Jesus.

My grandma Flo knew where God had brought me from, and that moment when she went with us to church brought joy to her life. She stayed with us for two months, and it was amazing. But eventually the time came for her to go back home. We all were saddened when she had to go, but we had to move forward with our life.

It was time for my kids to go to school, and I was going back to college as well. Life was moving in a great direction for my family. I kept my eye on God and I got (my family on a schedule. I put this daily schedule to action when our kids were really young:

- morning prayer
- breakfast/washing up for the day
- school/work
- homework/playtime
- dinner/TV time
- Bible stories/bed

I saw that it was working for our life. I saw that it brought peace and balance into our home. The kids were up from about 7:00 a.m. until 7:00 p.m., and by seven in the evening, my house was closed and cleaned. Our kids would watch TV in the evening, and then we would pray and read the Bible every night. My kids are older now, and our home is still like this. Even though they're not in the bed by seven, they know that the kitchen is closed at that time. With this schedule, my husband and I were able to have our time without the kids. We wanted to keep our marriage fresh. We had to make sure that we kept up with what happened during each other's days. This was my time to learn what I needed to pray about for my family.

I would get up earlier than my family so I could pray for our day. I would then make sure that my family members were ready for their day. I believed in the power of covering your family through prayer. This was the first year into our move. God was restoring my family. I could see the way God was moving, and it was beautiful. So in year two of our move, I asked myself what happened. How did we go from blessing to darkness within a year? I look back at that experience, and all I can think of is that we allowed too many people into our lives. I wish I'd known then how strong I really was in Christ and who Christ was in me.

God's word tells us in John 15:3–4, "Now ye are clean through the word which I have spoken unto you. Abide in me, and I in you. As branch cannot bear fruit of itself, except it abide in the vine; no more can ye, except ye abide in me."

Starting to Trust My Thoughts

As time went on, I found myself getting overwhelmed with my thoughts. On top of all that, I took on the responsibility of teaching Bible study and Sunday school. I was burning out fast. I found myself staying in my head, and eventually my thoughts started to take over. I became sad and cried all the time; something that was supposed to be a blessing started to feel like a curse. My life was unraveling quickly in front of me. I started to lose my focus on the very thing I prayed about. I was no longer smiling or enjoying college, and my life started feeling more chaotic. I kept going to school and teaching at church, though, because I didn't want to give up on myself. I wanted my kids to see me as a strong woman, even though I couldn't see myself as the strong woman I wanted to be. I put so much pressure on myself. I wanted to be like my friends. They were all so strong, and they knew it. I felt like a little girl trapped in a woman's body. I had painted a picture of how I was supposed to be, and now I was trying to be her. I struggled with my identity in Christ. I walked in so many things that God had never called me too.

I tried talking to my husband, but my words would always come out wrong. I never said the right things. I just wanted things to fall into place for me. I thought that if I told my husband about how I was feeling then he would listen to me. No. That was not how it would go for me. I always felt defeated, so I would pray. Then after praying, I would try to talk with my husband again. To him it I felt like I was nagging him, but I wasn't. I just wanted for him to be an ear. He never understood what I was saying or what I was really feeling on the inside.

This was the enemy's plan to cause division in our marriage. I knew that I needed to trust God with my life, but I was afraid to let go of my control. This became a major issue for me. I wanted to trust God so badly, but I began to put all my trust in my husband. I thought that if I could tell my husband my thoughts, that would make things better.

I read in 2 Corinthians 10:3–5 "though we walk in the flesh, we do not war after the flesh: (For the weapons of our warfare are not carnal, but mighty through God to the pulling down of strong holds;) Casting down imaginations, and every high thing that exalteth itself against the knowledge of God, and bringing into captivity every thought to the obedience of Christ." After reading this verse, I tried so hard to stop overthinking things. I just couldn't get myself to let go of control and to let God's will be done. I wrestled with this for a year—the tugging and pulling for control. It became my biggest downfall. During this time, I started to listen to people around me instead of to God.

I allowed my emotions to get the best of me, and I lost my focus on our life goals. I thought to myself, *My husband is supposed to be my strength.* I wanted him to be everything for me. I started to stress him out because I am a talker. I would go to him with everything; I just wanted him to listen to me. I thought that my husband was supposed to pick up my load for me. But when I did go to him, he would ask me, "Why are you doing all this? You don't have to do all this extra work at church."

Walking in Self-Condemnation

I took on all these responsibilities because I thought that was what God wanted me to do. I didn't want to make God mad at me because I wasn't being of service to him at church, but that was all lies of the enemy. I started to punish myself with guilt. I would tell myself, *You know that you can handle all this. You just want others to do it for you. Stop being a baby and grow up.* I was living with so much condemnation that I started to go back to my old way of thinking. Fear was one of the things that the enemy used on me all the time. I was scared of dying, and fear made me feel like God was going to allow me to die if I didn't do things right. I was so blinded by the lies of the enemy that I thought I was right and everyone else was out to get me.

I didn't want to tell people that I had no control over my thoughts. I was full of guilt, and condemnation, and on top of all that, I was now ashamed of myself and my life. I wanted to feel better. I wanted to be who God had called for me to be. I was trapped in a broken mindset. I just wanted that control back, so I started to pull back from friends at school and church. We left that church and started going to another church. But though I no longer had the responsibility of leading things in the new church, that didn't' change the way I was feeling on the inside. I was hurting and broken.

I started to believe all the lies that the enemy was telling me. I was the type of person who needed everything to look familiar to me. I needed that sense that it was going to be OK so that I could have peace in my mind. I believed in God, I loved God, and I was also scared of God. I feared God in an unhealthy way. I thought that he was going to punish me for everything.

An older woman told me one day about 1 John 4:18: "There is no fear in love; but perfect love casteth out fear: because fear hath torment. He that feareth is not made perfect in love." I was fearing God' punishment instead fearing out of love. My sins had me running away from God just like Adam and Eve did when they allowed their sin to separate them from the Father's love.

> And they heard the voice of the Lord God walking in the garden in the cool of the day: and Adam and his wife hid themselves from the Lord God amongst the trees of the garden. (Genesis 3:8)

I was pushing myself so hard that I didn't have anything for my family at the end of the day. This time it was a lot worse for me because I started to fight against God's plan for my life. Matthew 7:26-27 says, "But everyone who hears these words of mine and does not put them into practice is like a foolish man who built his on sand. The rain came down, the streams rose, and the winds blew and beat against that house, and it fell with a great crash"(NIV). When your foundation is not rooted and grounded in Christ Jesus, everything will be able to move you.

I Knew the Word

Though I knew Christ and was working in service to Christ, I had not surrendered to Christ. I was easily moved by everything that came my way in life. That was my major problem. I was not rooted in Christ to the point that God was enough for me. I still wanted everything to be about me. I wanted people to see me as a woman who had it all together, but on the inside, I was crying for help.

I brought trouble into my life because I wasn't trusting God with my life or my problems. During this time, I painted a fake picture for the world that I was perfect, that my life was perfect. But my whole life was a big fantasy. I just wanted to belong to something, so I joined everything I could at church so that it looked like I had it all together. That is a dangerous place to be. Not only can you hurt someone else, but you set yourself up to be hurt as well. I wanted so badly to be a strong woman in Christ, but I still wanted to be me as well. The two don't go well together at all.

My husband started to become angry at me, and I started to become angry at him. The devil had me believing that I could have everything I wanted. I didn't want much; all I wanted was to be heard and to be loved. I found myself hurting. I called pastor Jay, and he asked, "What have you done?" He told me that I had given my soul over to pastor Jones of the church we went to and that God was going to get both of us for that. I had entered into a mindset of depression. I put all my trust in man instead of God. As it says in Psalms 118:8–9, "it is better to trust in the Lord than to put confidence in man, it is better to trust in the Lord than to put confidence in princes." I had stopped trusting the God that was living on the inside of me due to fear. I didn't believe that God loved me anymore because of me. These were all lies that the enemy used against me for years.

The night before my darkest day came, my best friend LG called me and told me that God had said for me to plead the blood of Jesus over my family. I was so angry that I couldn't, and because of my disobedience, my world changed overnight. It was turned upside down. When we had left our church home, we'd started going and visiting other churches around the area. But now I stopped going altogether. Still, though all this was going on in my life, I somehow managed to finish college and graduate.

My life was a big disappointment for me. How had I gone from being made new to being in a place of brokenness. I was lost, but I knew that God was going to get the glory from all this mess that I had brought into my life. My pastor Jay started ministering to me again. He prayed for me like never before. My husband told me that we were going to move back to our home church in North Carolina, and I was so excited because I knew then I could get the help that I needed to get back to Christ.

So, we moved once again. My husband knew that he would be gone for several months for his job once we got back to our last duty station, so we visited my family before we made our move to North Carolina. But my life was not my life; I couldn't even enjoy our visit. I was so broken and lost that when I went to my mom's church one Sunday, I couldn't even stay for the whole service. I remember my husband looking at me and saying, "Let me get you out of here." He asked my mom if she would bring our kids home with her, and she said that she would. We left, and then my husband took me to the docks at the river by my parents' house.

My husband parked our SUV and began to talk with me, but his words could not help me at all. I got out of the car and started walking over toward the water. I thought that if I jumped in and died, then all my pain would be over, and I would finally be free. I stopped, though and thought about my kids and how they needed me. Then I turned back around and got back into our SUV. I just laid in the front seat crying because I really didn't know what to do about my pain. I was really good at hiding things from people to the point that my parents didn't know that anything was going on with me. My husband told me that I had to get better because our kids needed me. I wanted to get my life back, so my husband and I started praying every day while we were still on vacation. God delivered me from the spirit of suicide through our prayers.

When time came for our family to move into our new home, we left my parents' and started our journey. I had gotten to a place where I just prayed and fasted so that God could help me and forgive me for what I had done when I'd made our previous church my whole life. Our family started going to our home church, and our pastor Jay started to counsel my husband and me. God wanted to restore us so he could use us. At the same time, my husband was getting ready to leave.

We knew that God was going to help get our lives back on track, but it was going to take time and dedication from both of us. Even though my husband had to be away, God still had a plan for us. God's plan was bigger than both of us. So when the time came for my husband to leave, I wasn't sad, because I believed God was with us.

I kept working and going to church, and pastor Jay kept counseling me. He told me that he was not going to stop praying for me until God told him to. My kids and I started to enjoy the place that God had called us to. I would take them places every weekend, since I worked during the week. During one of my counseling sections with pastor Jay, he told me that my kids needed me but that I was in a place where I was trying to heal myself instead of letting God heal me from all my brokenness. I was masking the pain. That hit home because I loved my kids with all my being, but I was still holding on to the pain. Remember, I told you that I was good at hiding things, but there is nothing you can hide from the Holy Spirit. Pastor Jay knew that I was still hurting and that it was getting in the way of how I was parenting my kids. I thought that if I bought them things and kept them busy then I was a great mom because they were happy.

I was not going to just let the enemy continue to rob me and my family out of our lives, not another moment. I thank God for pastor Jay and his words because they gave me strength to take my life back from the enemy. I kept praying and started to praise God again. I was determined to take back my family. This was the family that I had prayed for, and they were worth the battle. I was in a war to take back my life, and I was not going to give up without a fight. I told myself, *If you can be fearless in this world fighting people, then you'd better be fearless in your fight with the enemy.* I bought a dry-erase board and wrote Psalms 91 on it. My kids and I would read this verse every night. We were praying over my husband with that verse. I wanted all my life back. I didn't want anything missing. My kids and I started hanging out at home more; we would have pizza and movie nights.

The enemy will keep you so busy that you can't see that there is even a problem. I started learning more about my kids and what they liked to do. I wanted to find out if there was something new going on in their lives that I needed to know. I started praying that

God would give me a job closer to our home because I worked about twenty minutes away. That meant that I was away from my kids all day long. I did not want that anymore. I want to be with my kids. I missed getting up, eating breakfast, and doing homework with them. If there was one thing that I knew, it was the power of fasting. Fasting will change everything.

One day at work I started writing to God on a piece of paper, telling God that I wanted this particular job that was closer to my house. There was a job fair, and I went for an interview. I then said to God, "Let your will be done."

I thought about my life and where it was heading. I asked to God help me. Please, God, help me. I started to repent of all my sins because I knew that it was my sins that were keeping me from God and I didn't want a broken relationship with God anymore. True beauty can come from ashes, because if I hadn't gone through the pain and the brokenness, I would never have been hungry for God like I was. I was ready for the fight to take back everything that the enemy had stolen from me.

CHAPTER 5

You're Going to Make It

I made it my everyday mission to get up and pray and praise God for his blessing and for how he had his hand on me. Weeks had gone past, and God was about to start moving things in my favor again. I got a voicemail and discovered that human resources was trying to get in contact with me about the job I had applied for. We played phone tag for hours until I just decided, hey, I am going to call them until I get someone. And I did.

When the lady got on the phone, I told her my name and why I was calling. She told me that I had been selected for the job that I had applied for. She offered me a job closer to my house and asked me when I could start. She told me that I had to give my current job two weeks' notice after I got off the phone with her. I went back to work and went to my boss to tell her what was going on and to let her know that I was going to be turning in my two-week notice by the end of the day.

The enemy will always try you when God has blessed you. My boss told me that she didn't think that I would be able to leave my job in that time frame. Wait, what? Come again? I asked her why not, and she said it was because she did not have anyone to replace me at that time. I was not about to let the enemy come in, so I left her office, started to praise God for his favor, and wrote my two-week notice anyway.

Later on that day, I got a phone call from my dad. He had called me to let me know that one of my loved ones had passed away and that he wanted me to come home. I went to my boss to let her know what had happened and that my dad wanted me to come home. She told me that she was sorry for my family's loss and that today could be my last day at work. She told me to go be with my family during this difficult time. I told her thank you, and she hugged me and told me that I was a great employee and that I would be missed. All I could do was say *Thank you, God, for your favor.*

Hidden Blessings

I didn't know that God was going to work this out for me that way, but what came next was a hidden blessing. My dad called me and said that I didn't have to come home after all. That meant that I had two free weeks before it was time to start my new job. I got to put both of my kids on the bus and take them off of the bus. God is so good. I was getting a chance to be the kind of mom that I wanted to be with my kids.

I got to spend the rest of my morning every day with God reading my Bible. I would turn on my Christian music and just get into the presence of God. My days were like this until my job started. My mind was healthy and awake. And then God did another amazing thing in those two weeks. He opened another door for me. I got placed in a new location that was only two minutes from my house.

God knew my heart and how I wanted to keep up with the new changes in my life. Pastor Jay was teaching me the ways of a godly lifestyle, and it was amazing. By the time my husband got home, I was a new woman. I still had some more things in me that needed to change. I knew that I wanted God, and I didn't play around with his time or his love for me.

My husband made it back home after being gone for seven months for his job. I am not going to lie to you, it was a struggle to have my husband back. It was not because I didn't love him or I didn't want him back. I had just gotten into a routine with our kids and with how I was running our home, and I knew things would have to shift. I didn't want life to go back to the old way again, but what I didn't know was that God had not just been working on me. God had been working on my husband at the same time. God is so good. It took me about a month to let go and enjoy the fact that I had my best friend back home with me again.

No More Fear

My family was back together, and our new life was good, until one day when I got into the shower and found a lump in my left breast. I called for my husband. He came into the bathroom, and I told him that I had found a lump. He touched it and asked me what I wanted to do. I told him that I was going to make a doctor's appointment to get it checked out. I called, and they gave me an appointment for that Saturday. When I went to that appointment, the doctor said that both of my breasts looked suspicious, and she ordered a mammogram for me.

I talked to everybody that I could to see if someone else had experienced something like this before. My mom and my sister both told me that it was a cyst because they'd had the same thing. Some people told me that it was from eating or drinking too much caffeine. My mind was troubled. I talked to a good friend of mine, and she said, "You always get scared and run away. Don't let fear get you again; trust God's plan for your life. Whatever it is, trust him with it."

Later on that evening, pastor Jay spoke with me and said, "You have to stay before God and go get your body checked out." He told me a story about when he had a cancer scare, and he encouraged me, telling me that God would not leave me but that I must trust him with my life.

God is so amazing. The doctor made me an appointment for a mammogram. I had just turned thirty years old a week before all this. The night before my appointment, my husband told me that he would go with me.

When the rest of my family all went to sleep that night, I sat in the hallway of where all our bedrooms were and started praying and asking God to spare my life. I had two children, and I wanted to see both of them grow up. I sat there and looked into both of their rooms as they slept, and I just wept for the simple fact that we didn't know what was going on with me. But I had to put all my trust in God and his plan, and I had to look fear in the eye and say, *No, I am not going to get scared this time.* God had given me peace.

I went to sleep, but it was soon time for me to get up for work. I went to work for a little bit that day, and then when time came for my appointment, I went home to pick up my husband. But what I didn't know was that our daughter had stayed home from school. I asked my husband why she was home, and he told me that she felt sick and that he wouldn't be able to go with me to my appointment. I was sad, but at the same time I was OK with it because he was home with our daughter.

God has a way of showing up in an area you never would expect. I went to my appointment with the lump still in my breast. Something strange happened to me as I got to the entrance of the hospital. This older guy, as he was leaving the hospital, looked at me and said smiling, "It's going to be all right." I smiled back at him and kept going to my appointment. As they got me ready for my mammogram, the nurse told me what they were going to do. She walked me through all the procedures. She said that if the doctor needed to get a closer look, then we would have to do a spot test and an ultrasound as well.

When they started my testing, I had this song by Hezekiah Walker in my spirit.

> I am reaping the harvest God promised me
> Take back what the devil stole from me
> And I shall rejoice today
> For I shall recover it all

I sang that song the whole time in my spirit while my test was being completed. I started to cry because I could feel the Spirit of the

Lord on me, but the nurses thought that I was crying because they were hurting me. One of the ladies asked me if that was the case, and I said, "No, it's OK."

When they got done with the testing, they took the pictures to my doctor and returned shortly after. They said that the doctor was asking for a spot test so he could get a better picture. Now this part of the test hurt really badly. They had to get my body into the right position so the picture would be clear for the doctor. They then took those pictures to the doctor and returned to tell me that the doctor was requesting an ultrasound. He needed a better view. By this time, I was starting to get scared, but I kept holding on to God's hand the whole time. It was like he was right there holding my hand back.

They took me into the ultrasound room. I asked one of the nurse's what she could see, but she said I'd have to wait for the doctor. When the doctor came into the room, he started the test. He asked me if I remembered where the lump was on my breast. I started to touch my breast in the spot. I could not find the lump at all. I told the doctor that it had been just there before I came. He told me that it looked to have been a cyst that had healed on its own. I said yes sir, and they told me that I was free to go. As I was walking down the hallway, I overheard my doctor talking to another doctor. She asked him how my appointment had gone, and he told her it had been a cyst. She replied, "That was good news for her." When I got into my car, I thought about the song that I'd sung while getting my test done. I hadn't known at the time that God was removing that lump from my breast. I believe that God will test you to see if you would still believe in him if his answer were different.

When I got home, I ran into the house, full of excitement about the miracle God had just done right before my eyes. I told my husband what the doctor had said, and of course he was like, "I told you that you would be fine, but you don't ever want to listen to me." We both smiled at each other. My daughter gave me a card that she had made while I was at the hospital. She had written on the card, thanking God for allowing me to be her mom. She thanked God for allowing me to be healed.

Who his own self bare our sins in his own body on
the tree, that we, being dead to sins, should live unto
righteousness: by whose stripes ye were healed. (1
Peter 2:24)

See, I'd never told our kids what was going on. That's why I was
blown away by her words; I knew they were from God.

I asked her how she was feeling, and she said, "I felt better after
Dad gave me some pickle juice."

"What! Pickle juice?" I said to her, laughing.

She said, "That's what daddy told me would help my stomach feel
better."

I gave my husband and our daughter the biggest hug ever. Then
I went into my garage and danced before God like David. I called
everyone and told them what God had done for me that day. I knew
that I was going to make it. God had favored me in my health, and I
was excited.

From that day forward, I started serving in our church. And I
wasn't the only one; my whole family started serving. I spoke with
pastor Jay about starting something for young girls, and he told me
that it was needed. He asked me if I knew what I would call the
ministry. God gave me the name Smart Girls For Christ, and we left
there to get everything in place for the new ministry.

I had to bring everything before the church, and that meant I had
to face another fear of mine: public speaking. I prayed and knew that
God would bring me through it. So when I got to church that Sunday,
I presented my new ministry, and everyone was very supportive; they
said that the church needed something like this for the girls. To my
surprise, a lot of the women at church wanted to be a part of the
ministry as well. I was so excited to get started, but my excitement
was short lived.

My husband got a new career opportunity that would ultimately
turn out to be a hidden blessing. But the new opportunity came with
a new location, and I was not happy at all. I had just gotten my life
together and was happy about what God was doing in my life. I was
finally about to start my new program at church. I spoke with pastor

Jay, and he told me to follow my husband. I didn't want to leave again to have to start all over again at a new church, so I wanted to fight against it. But God said, *Surrender. I will be with you.*

I figured that my assignment must be over there because we had just moved there a year and a half ago. I had to trust that God had reason for my family leaving this place so early. I stopped questioning God and started to trust him in this plan that I never saw coming. But God knew best. The purpose of this one move was to set my family up for the future. That's what I love about God; he will always set you up for a blessing, even when you can't see it.

I was reminded of God's word in Proverbs 3:5–8:

> Trust in the Lord with all thine heart; and lean not unto thine own understanding. In all thy ways acknowledge him, and he shall direct thy paths. Be not wise in thine own eyes: fear the Lord, and depart from evil. It shall be health to thy navel, and marrows to thy bones.

CHAPTER 6

Keeping the Faith

Once again, my family packed up for our new journey, but this time our new place was very familiar. It was my husband's hometown. I have learned that when God says that he is with you, he means what he says. The blessing didn't stop just because we moved. God opened doors that I'd thought were closed and that I'd never thought to reopen. I started asking God to help me with everything when it came to my life and my family. My husband and I agreed that I would stay home for a year so that I could get our family adjusted to the move. I thank God for this because God knew I would need it.

Shortly after our move, the Lord called pastor Jay, my spiritual father, home to be with him. The night before he passed away, I was sitting in my bedroom when I got a strong feeling that we needed to call him. I told my husband to call pastor Jay, and he said he would tomorrow. But I said, "No, call him now."

My husband asked for his number, so I gave it to him, and as soon as they got on the phone, they started laughing about something. I heard our pastor say, "That's your wife." Then my husband hung up the phone. I asked him why he hadn't let me talk with the pastor. I told him that I was going to call him back. My husband quickly told me no. He said the pastor was tired, so don't call him. But I called him anyway. I remember the pastor Jay laughing at me. We talked for a while, and I told him that I was coming back out there to see him in a couple of days. He told me to be safe, and as we got off the phone, I told him that I was praying for him and that I loved him. I never imagined that would be my last conversation with him.

God knew that he was going to call the pastor to come home, so he had to make a way for me to move when he did. God knew that it would have been too hard for me to stay. Pastor Jay always used to tell me that he would pray for me until God told him to stop. And right before we moved, he told me that he had stopped praying for me. He lifted his hands up before God with a praise, and I thanked God with him because I knew then that I was now where I was supposed to be with God.

I struggled with the fact that my spiritual father was gone. I knew pastor Jay would have wanted me to get up and keep moving in the Spirit of the Lord. I told myself to hold on to the pastor's legacy because he was a powerful man of God. He lived just that way before everyone.

I knew that I was ready to start back working, so I got a job quickly. But I knew early on that it wasn't the right job for me, so I left. I started praying for God to open up a door for me to get my dream job as a hairstylist. While I was waiting for the door to open, my family and I joined a new church and started to serve there. We knew that God wanted us to serve, and we jumped in quickly. I have learned that not all pastors teach the same, and I had to stop comparing my former pastor and spiritual father to the new pastor that we were now joined with. Even though their styles were different, the Word of God was the same. I got adjusted and started applying everything that I had learned.

I'd spent many years trying to find my place in life. I never was a quick learner, but this time things were different. I had now gotten a desire in my spirit. I wanted to change, and I knew I needed to change if I was going to serve God like he was calling me too.

Pushing Me into Position

I kept my focus on God and his plan for my life because trouble was knocking at the door. My husband's grandma had gotten sick. I went to visit her at the rehabilitation center, and she told me to read Psalms 23 to her. After I finished, she told me to read it again, and again. After the fifth time, she told me to stop. See, she was getting me to read it in the spirit because she was about to petition God for her life.

After I read the psalms, she told to me pray. I have never prayed like I did that day. She was teaching me how to usher in the Holy Spirit through prayer. I watched her ask God to give her a little more time because she had to get her family together, and from that day forward, she was on a mission to do just that. That was in August 2013. God graced her with more time as she asked, and in February 2014, when her assignment was complete, God called her home in peace.

Before she died, she told me that God had shown her my heart, and she never allowed anyone or anything to get in the way of our relationship. When she passed away, I was so sad because I knew that I was going to miss our relationship and, most of all, our talks. I held on to everything that she had deposited into me. During the time that God had given her grace to stay longer with us, I saw God move in ways that only God could. The way my husband's grandma would speak to her family, it was like she would minister to them in that area that they needed help in. It was amazing to hear her speak.

Now two amazing people who had been praying for me to make it in Christ had been called home. I had to keep the faith and hold on like never before to all their teaching and their wisdom. I knew they both were smiling down on me, so I kept smiling and working. But we all know that the enemy doesn't keep things quiet for long; he will always try something if you let him—sometimes even when you don't let him.

Deciding to Walk in Healing

I made a major decision to change my view on life. I knew that God was in me and that I was growing in Christ. I read my Bible all the time and prayed for God to give me understanding of his word.

I knew that I had to stay in prayer if I was going to be the woman God designed me to be. There were days that I had to pray harder because the old person was still very present in my life. I had not yet separated myself all the way from my former sinful self. I knew that the more I stayed in God's presence, the more his word would cleanse and change me. I wanted God to change me for his glory, I knew that I had to do my part as well. I knew this change was not going to happen overnight. I was going to have to be strong.

> Knowing this, that our old man is crucified with him, that the body of sin might be destroyed, that henceforth we should not serve sin. For he that is dead is freed from sin. (Romans 6:6–7)

Even at work I tried to stay away from unholy conversations. I knew I was in a place of change. This was not always easy because sometimes I would be asked a question that would trigger something inside of me. I would allow myself to get caught up in these kinds of conversations until one day when God's word convicted my heart. All I could do was pray for forgiveness. I learned that when you ask God for something, you have to believe that he will do it. My problem was not always that I joined the conversations; it was that I stayed around ungodly conversations. I had to have a change in my mindset if I was going to know how to walk away from the temptation.

> Let no corrupt communication proceed out of your mouth, but that which is good to the use of edifying, that it may minister grace unto the hearers. (Ephesians 4:29)

I got to a point in this job that I was ready to leave it, but God had a bigger plan for me. I didn't have the patience to wait for God during this season of my life, however. God wanted me to stay there because he was teaching me in this trial, but I didn't want to listen. I left the job as a hair stylist anyway. I thought that I had found a better job—one that came easy to me—but this was one of the biggest mistakes ever.

The enemy didn't show me the trial that I was going to enter into at this new job. It was far worse than the trial I'd endured at the last one.

The enemy will only show you a lie, and I believed his lie. God loved me even in my disobedience, though. I had to go through this trial that I was facing, but God didn't leave me alone. He was right there with me, helping me stand on his word. I wish I would have just waited on God to fix my problems at my last job as a stylist. In that lesson, I would have learned how to handle myself as a businesswoman.

I left my dream job as a hair stylist because I was impatient. I thought that God wasn't moving fast enough for me. I had to learn the hard way that God is an orderly God and that in him there are no sorrows. I was still about the self; I had to be broken of that self-focused spirit that I had been walking in for years.

When God brought me out of the trial from my job at the care center, I knew it was God and only God. I came out of that trial with a change of mind; I believed that God was with me. God not only delivered me from the enemy's hand, but he also closed the door for me working in that field of work. God called me to come out of this job and never to go back to it again.

> Hear my cry, O God; attend unto my prayer. From the end of the earth will I cry unto thee, when my heart is overwhelmed: lead me to the rock that is higher than I. For thou hast been a shelter for me, and a strong tower from the enemy. (Psalms 61:1–3)

Though God had delivered me from this, he was about to deliver me from years of bondage. I was about to really see who God was in my life. Shortly after leaving that job at the care center, God opened a door that neither my husband nor I wanted or had ever wanted to go through. God was sending us back to Japan. We fought against this for months until we both said, "I guess this is where we are going." God had a plan for my life. He knew I was ready this time, and I couldn't run away from it.

> Being confident of the very thing, that he which hath begun a good work in you will perform it until the day of Jesus Christ. (Philippians 1:6)

God was about to take me through the process of attaining my true deliverance in him. This was not going to be easy, but I prayed and fasted before even leaving for this journey. I knew that God was with us, because he was sending me back to Japan, a place where I had been broken and wounded by words that had altered my life. I learned through all my teaching that the Holy Spirit was calling me to pray without ceasing.

CHAPTER 7

Coming Full Circle in My Life

As we were making plans to move, we were also making plans for coming back. We wanted to get this move over with quickly. For me, this was a difficult move. When I was nineteen years old, I'd run from this place. I didn't know if the same struggles were waiting for me on my return. This transition made me go deeper into the Word of God. I stayed in my secret closet with the Father.

> That thine alms may be in secret: and thy Father which seeth in secret himself shall reward thee openly. (Matthew 6:4)

When time came for us to move in with my parents for two weeks, I used that time for prayer. Every morning at 6:00 a.m., I would go into my parents' den with my Bible and my journal. I told myself, *You will be ready this time when God calls you.* There were things in my past that I had to face, and it would not be easy. But I was ready to let go of all my past so I could live without the residue of my struggles.

I kept myself away from negative people during this time of waiting and kept speaking the Word of God.

During this two-week period, we got to spend time with our loved ones. This was an amazing moment for us. We got so many words of encouragement from everyone. I got to have a special moment with a loved one that would change my view on fighting the good fight; during our time in Japan, she left to be with her King. That's why it was good to be still waiting for the move. If I would have just ripped and run around visiting, I would have missed the gift God gave us: the gift of saying goodbye.

> But they that wait upon the Lord shall renew their strength; they shall mount up with wings as eagles; they shall run, and not be weary; and they shall walk, and not faint. (Isaiah 40:31)

Saying Goodbye

As the hugs and tears came, we had to trust that God had everything in his hands. Before we got into the car, my auntie told me to hurry back so we could celebrate all that God was going to do. Saying goodbye was not easy. When we got to the airport, I was scared on the inside because I hated flying on airplanes. But I couldn't let that fear take over. I told myself, *You have to be strong for your kids now. You have to be the one to hold their hands when they get scared.*

As I held their hands, my husband was holding my hand as well because God had given me a husband that loved his family. My husband reassured me that this was not just the closing of a major chapter in our lives; it was also the start of a new chapter that was going to be the best yet. I held on to my husband's words as we got onto all our flights.

When we got to our destination, I was fighting back tears and all the fears that I was feeling. My kids, though, were so excited that they were moving somewhere different. They were ready for all the fun and exciting trips we told them we would take them. I was not about to go backward in my faith at all. I stayed in prayer. I wrote in my prayer journal daily, and I stood on God's truth. God had trained me up for this, even though I had no clue in the process. I trusted God through it all. I told myself these words daily: "Let this mind be in you, which was also in Christ Jesus" (Philippians 2:5).

Learning about True Discipleship

We had been there on the island for about a month and had started going to church. It was good. I was so hungry for God's Word and everything that he was doing inside of me.

> Blessed are they which do hunger and thirst after righteousness: for they shall be filled. (Matthew 5:6)

I told my husband that I wanted to do something with the youth at church, and he told me to go for it. So the following week when we went to Bible study, I spoke with the pastor. I told him some backstory about my journey with wanting to start a ministry just for young girls. He told me to visit this local youth ministry that had been created by a husband and wife. They hosted a small group once a week for people who wanted to start working with the ministry. I was so excited that I didn't miss a week. The group was so amazing; they all offered so much important information about ministry.

I was so sad when we came to the last of the small-group meetings. I had come to love being with people who had the same hunger I did for doing God's work in ministry. I went back to the pastor, and he connected me with another woman who wanted to be a part of the ministry as well. I prayed that God would show me what he wanted me to do, and he showed me not to move forward in the ministry— not yet.

God was telling me to be still. I knew from my previous trials that when God speaks, you'd better listen. I kept trusting in the Lord with everything he was saying and doing in my life. So, I went to my husband about opening up a beauty salon. I wanted to open it up in our home. My husband was OK with that, and he helped me get started. He bought all the materials that I would need for my salon.

I was excited for his support. I got my home all set up and got all my business cards made.

Lies from the Enemy

As things started to go well for me, the enemy decided to show up again by putting negative thoughts in my head: *You're not the best. There are so many women on this island that are better than you are. You're not going to make it. Nobody's going to want to get their hair done by you.* And so on.

I kept remembering my auntie's words, that they were going to celebrate my success when we got back. I had to start believing in myself because everyone in my life was believing in me. When my son was out playing, he would tell his friends' parents that I did hair and would give them our address so they could come and speak to me. I got most of my clients because of my son. I had no room for fear or doubt because my baby boy believed in me, and he wanted me to be successful. He would tell me, "Mom, I am proud of you."

In the beginning, though, my daughter was my one and only client. I kept her hair done so that people would see it and compliment it. That way she could promote my business. I wanted her to tell people to come to my hair salon, but she did not want me to do other people's hair at all. She believed in me, but she was like, "You are my hair stylist, and I don't want to share you because if you get too busy, you won't have any time to do my hair." I reassured her that I wouldn't let that happen at all because I loved her too much to let it happen.

God has given me an amazing support system through my family's love. As time went on, I would think only of the things of God. I started praying more with my kids every night, and we kept going to church and Bible study as a family. For my husband and I, our true foundation is Christ. We wanted Christ to be the center of our family. We would bring other people to church with us as well. I started getting more clients, and I was starting to make a name for myself.

There was a part of me that still wanted to be back home with my family. God even took care of that by soon sending my nephew

Marquis overseas with us. I serve a God who cares about every small detail of his children's lives. I was so thrilled for my nephew to be in the same place as my family. We did so much together. God knew how much I love my whole family, and spending time with them was priceless at times. My nephew Marquis even started to come with us to church. I was determined to share my faith with everyone I knew— even those that I didn't know. Life was good. I had my family with me, and my relationship with Jesus was growing stronger.

> Ye are the light of the world. A city that is set on a hill cannot be hid. Neither do men light a candle, and put it under a bushel, but on a candlestick; and it giveth light unto all that are in the house. Let your light so shine before men, that they may see your good works, and glorify your Father which is in heaven. (Matthew 5:14–16)

I made a mental note to remind myself that every time that I would get comfortable, the enemy would try to come in to see if I was weak. So, I kept with my studies, and I kept sharing God's truth. As God started to let my business grow, I started having issues with my health. The first time I knew something was wrong was the day I went to pick up Marquis. I think it was during the fall. I didn't understand why this was happening to me. See, this was the beginning of my deliverance.

The Beginning of the Breaking

I did not know what was going on, but God did. My health issues went on for about a week before I finally went to the hospital. That day I went out to the store, and when I got into my car, I started feeling the thing that had been bothering me. It felt like I was having an asthma attack. I called my husband at work and started crying as he answered the phone. He asked me what was wrong, and I told him how I was feeling. I told him that I couldn't take it anymore feeling like this. He told me to just go to the hospital to get checked out.

I had a new client scheduled for that day and had to call her to cancel because I had to head to the doctor. When I got to the ER, they took me in the back. The doctor said that he could see that my throat was irritated. He gave me a drug cocktail to numb my throat, but he said that it wouldn't fix the underlying problem. It would just help with the irritation that I was feeling.

This went on for about two months, off and on. Every time it happened, I would go back to the ER. On my last visit to the ER, the doctor told me that he was going to make an appointment for me with my doctor. He told me that she would be able to do more tests to see what was really going on with me. As I waited to see my doctor, I started writing in my prayer journal. I sang praises to God for everything that he was doing for me. I repented of any sins that I had committed without knowing. I would get up early in the morning to pray.

I was still pushing through life; I was not going to give up at all. I knew God had not brought me this far to leave me now. When time came for me to see my doctor, she asked me what was going on. I started telling her everything that I was experiencing. She looked at me and said, "You have new allergies." She said that some people come to the Island and have no problem with their allergies, and some people like me have a harder time with their allergies.

> Every branch in me that beareth not fruit he taketh
> away: and every branch that beareth fruit, he purgeth
> it, that it may bring forth more fruit. (John 15:2)

My doctor gave me some allergy medicine and sent me on my way. I thanked God the whole way home. I called my husband and told him what I'd learned at my appointment. My husband has always told me that I would be OK.

I took my medicine and started feeling like myself again. I kept getting up early to praise God, and I kept moving in the Spirit. Though it seems like I never listen, I really do. It is a process for me at times. One thing I do know is that I am a fighter, and I was not giving up, because I knew where my help comes from. God was breaking me away from everything that had me in bondage. I knew God was busy at work inside of me. I had no reason to be afraid anymore. My best friend LG's husband told me that God had me in the safety of his hands. LG was always praying for me and she and I would pray together once a week over the phone to this day we still call each other once a week.

> Peace I leave with you, my peace I give unto you: not
> as the world giveth, give I unto you. Let not your heart
> be troubled, neither let it be afraid. (John 14:27)

CHAPTER 8

No More Running

I started out my morning with God at 5:00 a.m., praying and praising. I knew the only way I was going to get to my victory place in God was to stay before him. I started taking back some of my clients and started calling my family back home more. I also started to have Bible studies every night with my kids because I wanted them to have a relationship with God—not just any relationship, but a healthy relationship.

I knew God was up to something, because out of the blue my husband was told that he would be leaving the island for two weeks. God knew I didn't like being without my husband. I started to get stressed out to the point that I was not focused at work. I started doing back-to-back services, but I knew the condition of my hands wouldn't allow me to continue. Two days before my husband left, I irritated my right hand. I was in so much pain that I went to the doctor, and the doctor did a strength test on me. That test showed that I had lost five percent of my strength in that hand.

The doctor gave me some exercises to do at home to help with loosening up the nerve in my hand. I was mad at myself for having allowed this to happen. I had to stop doing hair because of it, and doing hair had always been my dream. My heart was heavy, but I was feeling so much pain from my hand that I just had to take a break from my dream job.

In this moment of pain, I took my eyes off of God and put them on my problem. This led me to become overwhelmed with my emotions. I only thought about my pain all day long. I tried so hard to get my joy back, but nothing was working.

The Turnaround

I went to church feeling so fed up with living with defeat every day of my life. I told myself that I was not going to leave that church until God set me free. I stayed after the service was over and just stood in the sanctuary crying. One of the elders asked me if I wanted him to get one of the women from the church to pray for me, and I said yes. He came back with his wife and three other women. They all circled around me and started praying over me. The mother of the church told me to open my mouth and praise God; she told me that the Word of God was in me and that now I had to bring it up. I started speaking over myself with the Word of God. In that moment as they prayed, I was able to feel the anointing that was in that place.

After they were done praying with me, the mother of the church hugged my neck and spoke words that changed my view of life forever. She said, "You know the Word of God, and you'd better open up your mouth and speak those words over yourself. You'd better not let me see you like this again. You'd better stop acting like you don't know who God is inside of you." She spoke with power. The Holy Spirit broke that heaviness off of me to the point that I actually began to feel lighter. I left the church that day as a different person. My hunger for the word of God was different from that point on. I made it my business not to come back to church in that state of mind again. Every morning I laid out before God's feet. I started dancing before God until things started falling off of my life.

My joy returned back to me from that day forward. When my husband returned home, he noticed that I was different. Every day I would lift up my hands and dance before God. Now that my life had changed for the better, I made a decision to serve God all the days of my life. I started looking for a part-time job just to get out of the house for a couple of hours of the day. I got the job, and I changed the way I was living and started thanking God for everything.

This all happened within the second year of us living overseas. I told myself that God had brought me back to Japan to face my fears so I could stop running from the calling that was on my life. I was broken, and I just wanted to get out of it, but God said to me, *You must go through the fire this time.* I had nowhere to hide; everything about me was exposed before God. All I wanted was for God to hurry up this part of the process. I told myself that the pressure was too much for me to handle. I thought that I was going to die. But God said, *You are not going to die but live.* One of my good friends Tasha told me, "You're not leaving here until your work is done."

> That the trial of your faith, being much more precious than of gold that perisheth, though it be tried with fire, might be found unto praise and honour and glory at the appearing of Jesus Christ. (1 Peter 1:7)

What Was Broken

Three things were broken in my life:

1. Fear was broken off of me. I spent all my twenties and most of my thirties in bondage. There were times that God would show me that I had a love issue. I would try so hard to get back to the way I used to love. God had to show me that fear was keeping me from experiencing the Father's love. Fear was causing me to hide with anxiety, doubt, and worrying.

> For God hath not given us the spirit of fear; but of the power, and of love, and of a sound mind. (2 Timothy 1:7)

2. Self-condemnation was broken off of me. God delivered me from beating myself up daily. This was an uphill battle for me; I thought that

I was never good enough. I had to be broken free from the words that had been spoken over me by people who I trusted the most. There is a saying that we have as children: sticks and stone may break my bones but words will never hurt me. These are lies; words have the ability to alter your view of who God called you to be.

> Even so the tongue is a little member, and boasteth great things. Behold, how great a matter a little fire kindleth! (James 3:5)

3. Envy was broken off of me. For years of my life, I was taught to compare myself to others. I'd never thought there was anything wrong with this part of my life, but because of envy, I struggled with who God had called for me to be. I always tried to be like other people. I remember one day praying for God to bless me; God's response to me was *Who are you asking me to bless? I won't bless this person that you are trying to be, but I will bless the person that I called you to be.*

> For we dare not make ourselves of the number, or compare ourselves with some that commend themselves: but they measure themselves by themselves, and comparing themselves, are not wise. (2 Corinthians 10:12)

Small Group Changed My Life

I had no place to hide or run anymore. I had to face my truth, and it wasn't easy at all. But I was determined to live my life just the way God had called me to. I joined a small group at church. It was amazing to be a part of a group of women whose main mission was to support other women in their Christian walks. We read a book called *Unashamed* by Christine Caine. I did not want to read only the chapters that were assigned to us. I couldn't put the book down, I wanted to finish it in one day. I read Christine Caine's book, and chains began to fall off of me. I did not have to be ashamed of my past anymore.

While this session of the small group was going on, my husband had to leave the island again, but I was changed mentally. When the day came for my husband to leave, I dropped him off at the airport. I then came home and jumped right into devotion. When it came time for me to get my kids ready for school, I quickly sent them on their way; I wanted to get back into my book because I had a small group session that morning and was ready to enjoy myself with the other wives.

I got myself on a schedule at this time where from five to six thirty in the morning, I would do my devotions. I still follow this routine to this day.

The Journey of My Baptism

Time went by so quickly. A week had already passed by, and there was only one more week before my husband would come home. I spent hours reading my word and praying in the Spirit. I remember the moment I spoke to God about getting rebaptized. I knew what the word says about one baptism, but I told God that I wanted to do that part of my life right. When I'd gotten baptized earlier in my life, I really didn't understand it. I'd just been told that it was the next step when you got saved. Now I wanted to right all my wrongs.

I spoke with the elders of my church about my decision to get rebaptized, and they reminded me of the word about one baptism. I told them that I understood but that there were some things in my life that I had to fix and that this was one of them. They asked if I understood what this meant. I told them yes. They asked me when I wanted to do this. I told them the next Sunday because my husband would be back home the Friday before. I then spoke with my husband about my decision, and he was supportive like always. I told him that my plan was to have my baptism on Sunday since he was coming home on Friday night.

Speaking God's Word

Later on that week, my husband called me and said that he didn't know when he would be back home. There was something wrong with the flights. I told him that we were going to trust God and speak the Word of God only. I believed God was going to work it out for us. I prayed, and I trusted God. When Friday came, my husband called me to tell me that he would be coming back home on Saturday. I started shouting and praising God. I told my husband, "See, all we had to do was believe."

On Saturday, I learned that his plane was running late. I started praying hard to Jesus because we needed him. The plane arrived a little bit after midnight, but we still had to wait at the airport until everybody was able to leave. We finally made it home at about one thirty Sunday morning. We got little to no sleep, but I was excited to have my family with me on this journey. We got up and headed to the beach, where I got baptized. It was an amazing experience that I wouldn't change. My family got to experience this journey with me, and they were so proud of me.

God is a good God. No more running for me; I was running to God. After my baptism, we went back home so we could get ready for church. It was my week to teach Sunday school to the older youth class. One thing that I have learned about myself is that even though I would run from trouble, I had a fight in me that would never let me give up on myself or my walk in Christ.

> If ye continue in the faith grounded and settled, and be not moved away from the hope of the gospel, which ye have heard, and which was preached to every creature which is under heaven; Whereof I Paul am made a minister. (Colossians 1:23)

I love God so much that I just want to be like him. I would watch all my friends and their walks with Christ, and they all gave me strength to hold on to God. I was growing, and I was learning just who I was in Christ Jesus. I was coming out of the fire knowing that

God knew my name I was God's daughter and I knew it my heart. I was learning about my adoption as a child of God.

The peace that I was now walking in because of God's word and his love was priceless. I wish I could have walked in God's understanding earlier in my life. This was a part of my journey; God knew that I would come to him. I didn't focus on how long it took me to let go in Christ Jesus but rather on the fact that I did let go.

> And not only they, but ourselves also, which have the firstfruits of the Spirit, even we ourselves groan within ourselves, waiting for the adoption, to wit, the redemption of our body. (Romans 8:23)

CHAPTER 9

Deliverance

My life was in God's hands, and I was walking with him. I was no longer troubled by my past. Small group helped me to understand that we all want to please God, but we need that sense of community to support us. We cannot live out our Christian lives without the right people; we need people who will be encouraging to others and help them with a willing hand.

God had to reteach me how to live my life with no condemnation. That was one of my issues. I always thought God was mad at me and that he was going to kill me for everything I did. That was a lie that the enemy was feeding me for years, and I believed him. I started to study the Word of God instead of just reading the Word of God; there is a major difference. I stopped working so I could just focus on the things that God was calling me to.

> Study to shew thyself approved unto God, a workman that needeth not be ashamed, rightly dividing the word of truth. (2 Timothy 2:15)

Breaking Chains

My kids were so happy. They told me, "Mom, we don't like it when you have to work and be away from our home." I was now enjoying the blessing of being a woman of God, a wife, and a mom. I'd wanted this life for so long, and I finally got to live it.

I started teaching my family all the things that I was learning about God and how we can live a holy life in this world. I bought Bible dictionaries and I bought the concordant Bible to help me with my Bible studies. My family was now benefiting from the blessing of Go because I had gotten myself together. What a difference it can make when one person says yes to the Lord. I was healthy.

After about a month, my family decided to worship God from home. It was great because I got to study the Bible all day. It became a part of my life. I wanted to give my family the truth about God. We worshipped from home for months, and I could see a change the Word of God was making in my home. But after several months of me teaching, God spoke to my daughter and told her it was time to get out of the house. My daughter came and told me how she was feeling. She said, "Mom, you have been teaching from home for months, but God wants us to go to a church outside of our home."

Preparing for My Deliverance

My daughter talked to me in April 2018. See, Jesus always has a plan, because in March 2018, the Holy Spirit had told me to fast for thirty days. My life was about to change. The thing that had held me back from serving God was about to be broken forever.

So in April, my family went to a local church that morning, but today was not the average get-up-and-go-to-church kind of day. It became the day of my full deliverance! I was praying for my husband, but God had another plan—and it was for me. The Spirit of the Lord spoke to me and said, *Where the Spirit of the Lord is there is liberty.* After that, the Holy Spirit entered me, and I danced in that church like never before. The pastor ended church, but I was still dancing. One of the women from church told me to sit down and let the Holy Spirit minister to me. I heard the Holy Spirit say, *Feed my sheep.*

After I was able to calm down in the Spirit, I kept hearing *feed my sheep.* I lifted up my hand and answered with a "Yes, Lord!" I kept telling the Lord "Yes!" and the tears came down. Those tears were cleansing my soul. The lady put me into my husband's arms so he could hold me as God released me from all those years of bondage.

That marked the beginning of my true Christian walk as a *free woman in Christ*! See, that was just the beginning. Now the truth had begun to come out. I was learning to defeat the enemy, because Christ was now in his rightful place in my life and the teaching was clear from that point on. The teaching was evident that Christ was who he said he would be in my life. I was ready to go through the process because I was hearing the voice of the Holy Spirit, which was about to guide me through the difficult spots. The Holy Spirit reminded me of the word of the Lord: that he would never leave me nor forsake me. I knew and I believed for the first time that Jesus was with me. Jesus showed me how he had his angels around me protecting me every step of the way. What I thought would have been painful became the most beautiful experience of my life. I felt like it was the day I was born, and it was! It was the day I was born again.

Waking into my freedom became a journey of finding out that God was calling me and preparing me to teach his word. My studies became who I was. I learned how to break down God's word with understanding. I started to understand how to live out the word of God. I no longer caused my Christian walk to be difficult. I got into a healthy place with God, and I surrendered my will to God's will.

I'd had a major issue with submission, and because of that one issue, it took me years to be able to submit to a God who loves me unconditionally. I fought God for years for no reason at all. I ran from his perfect will for my life. I wanted, God but I wanted him on my terms. I didn't want to miss out on something I thought that I could get on my own. I had to surrender to God on so many levels, like when it came to being a wife. I'd never wanted to let go of my control. I'd thought that I would lose my voice and lose the person I was before I got married, which was the wrong way of thinking. God has given me an amazing husband. He's not perfect but he is perfect for me. It is a choice I have to make daily to stay before God. So now I read God's words in truth, and I have stopped leaning on my own understanding.

During this season of life, while we were still overseas, we lost two more family members. But before they left us, God blessed my family to be able to take a trip back to the States. We got to spend time with our two loved ones who are now angels. God kept his loving arms around us during this period of our lives. We serve a God who cares so much about us that he gave his only Son for our ransom.

I no longer try to fit into this world or care about the things of this world because I want to live for God. He has already given me so much to be thankful for, and I am going to praise him. I am so glad that God grabbed me out of my own way. He set me free from my own mindset of pain, disappointment, shame, hatred, and anger, as well as self-condemnation. I serve a God who loves me so much. I am reminded every day of his love and reminded that I cannot go far without it. I get to really enjoy my life knowing that God has me in his hands, and nothing can take me out them. It is a blessing just knowing the fact that you don't have to be in a battle every day.

I have many people in my life who want to see me do good in Christ. Not only is heaven cheering me on, but God has placed a circle of beautiful people around me to cheer me on as well. I am free to love other people. I am free to sing. I am free to dance. I am free because the Son has set me free. Amen!

During this process of deliverance, God was cleansing me. God had me study his Word constantly. He instructed me to read certain passages in John, including chapters 3, 6, 10, 11, 15, 16, and 21. God kept me in this teaching for months. I talked to a friend, and she told me that God was getting me prepared to share his Word with others. She encouraged me to keep with my studies. I stayed right there until God took me to other scriptures.

During this time, my husband had to leave the island again. This time we got hit by a typhoon and experienced three days of bad weather while he was away. The whole Island was shut down, and no one could go anywhere at all. My kids and I prayed, and God gave us peace. So we enjoyed every moment. We played board games and watched movies. The kids made their own breakfast pizza. We had a blast. Those moments were priceless. When the time came that we could finally leave our home, we went outside to see what everything looked like. It was a mess out there, but in my home, it was peaceful and full of joy. I give God all the glory for bringing me into a place of total peace and calm.

Once my husband came back home, I bought a new couch and chairs for the house. Let me take you back: God blessed my family to be able to go back to the States for three weeks. While we were in the States, I told God that material things didn't matter to me anymore. I never thought that we would experience mold damage after telling God that, but we came back home to a house full of moldy furniture. We had to throw away about 75 percent of our home. So, we sat on lawn chairs and a futon. Even though all these things had happened to us, we still kept our joy. We knew it was not about the materialistic things; it was about God and how he kept us safe. Still, after the typhoon was over, my kids and I decided that we needed something comfortable to sit on. We knew at that point that we didn't have much longer on the island before it was time for us to head back to the States, but we still wanted to be comfortable until that time came.

Time passed, and finally, after living overseas for three years, it was time for us to make our way back to the States. I was filled with excitement because I was leaving as a free woman in Christ Jesus. Even though my journey had been filled with ups and down and a lot of setbacks, I had not given up. I had remained hopeful that I would be set free and live the kind of life that God had for me.

I am grateful for all the people that God has placed in my life along the way. Some have been seasonal people who were there to plant a seed into my life. Others were sent to be lifelong friends. Not only did they help with planting God's seed into my life, but they also got to watch every one of those seeds start to grow up inside of me because of God's mighty hand of protection watching over me.

God is the Alpha and the Omega, the Beginning and the End. He knew just how long it would take me to fully get to a place where I was ready to receive him as my true Lord and savior.

I am grateful to God for allowing me to be a part of his family and to have received his forgiveness of my sins.

My best is yet to come!

CHAPTER 10

Separating Yourself

After years of longing for a change to come into my life, just like that, God showed up. There was no more playing around for me, no more hoping for something magical to drop down and change me. This was real. I could breathe without worrying about how things were going to be for me. God was now calling me to a place of separation; he was teaching me how to let go. This process of letting go was not easy at all. When I heard God's voice telling me to separate myself from certain things and people, I prayed that God would give me peace with this assignment. Some of these people had been in my life for years. But I knew that if God was calling me to this place, it meant that he was going to be with me. As I listened to God's voice, he led me to Romans 8. God broke this chapter down for me as I started to separate myself.

> There is therefore now no condemnation to them which are in Christ Jesus, who walk not after the flesh, but after the Spirit. (Romans 8:1)

During this time, God had me write letters to my friends to apologize for all my behavior. God was not just going to heal and deliver me; God was going to restore friendships that had been damaged along the way. One of my closest friends responded with so much love that it brought tears to my eyes. "My heart was full after reading her response to my apology". I cried for about an hour because God cared so much about my friendships.

> For the law of the Spirit of life in Christ Jesus hath made me free from the law of sin and death. (Romans 8:2)

God knew my heart and knew how I wanted to make everything right in my life. See, when God gives you permission to take back everything that the devil has stolen from you, he doesn't leave anything undone. God gave me restoration, joy, peace, forgiveness, and so much more. I did not play around with taking everything back out of the enemy's hand. I did it with joy, knowing that my Father had fought for me and for everything to be returned back to me with nothing lacking at all.

> For the Lord God is a sun and shield: the Lord will give grace and glory: no good thing will he withhold from them that walk uprightly. (Psalms 84:11)

My process of finding out who I was in Christ Jesus was a life-changing experience that was worth it. God was guiding me through the hardest places in my life so I could take back my birth right, which I had been giving away due to fear.

> Stand fast therefore in the liberty wherewith Christ hath made us free, and be not entangled again with the yoke of bondage. (Galatians 5:1)

These changes did not happen overnight; it took time before I was totally separated from everything. I thought the process would be scary, but God was walking with me, lighting my way through.

> Thy word is a lamp unto my feet, and a light unto my path. (Psalms 119:105)

During my thirty-day fast, God was showing me how to separate myself from certain foods. I had a sweet tooth that was out of this world, but now even that sweet tooth is gone. God was teaching me how to get healthy and stay healthy. I once heard a preacher say that God wants us to be healthy; that way there is nothing stopping us from fully serving God. I even became a vegan for a short time, but though I lost some weight with the lifestyle, it became too much for me. My husband started helping me in this area. He invited me to exercise with him daily. God was restoring us through our exercising. He was showing me how to let my husband take the lead.

> For the husband is the head of the wife, even as Christ is the head of the church: and he is the saviour of the body. (Ephesians 5:23)

When it came to watching TV and listening to music, God was changing all that too. I love watching TV and listening to different kinds of music, but God was teaching me to be careful of what I watched and listened to.

> Ye did run well; who did hinder you that ye should not obey the truth? This persuasion cometh not of him that calleth you. A little leaven leaveneth the whole lump. (Galatians 5:7–9)

God was saying to me, *If you leave these things in your life, they will grow into something that will become a stronghold.* God had delivered me, and I was not going to let TV shows or worldly music cause me to stumble again. I knew where God had brought me from, so I let go of it all. When I was around people who were watching something or listening to something that I didn't agree with in my spirit, I removed myself if I could. If there were times when I couldn't leave, I would tune out everything by opening up a good conversation.

When it came to parenting, God had to show me that I was holding on to my kids too tightly, that he couldn't be their God because of my grip. I have two kids who are very different in everything. This meant the way I was handling them had to change. I could no longer talk with them or punish them in the same way. I had to learn their ways and their personalities, and this meant I had to be still and quiet so that I could hear my kids and what they needed from me as their mom.

> Wherefore, my beloved brethren, let every man be swift to hear, slow to speak, slow to wrath. (James 1:19)

I became very watchful and prayerful in this area with them. What worked for one of my kids did not work for the other child. God grew my relationship with my children, even though my kids and I had already been close. God had to show me to trust him with their lives as well. I had to trust that they were listening to everything we were teaching them. This meant they were free to make their own mistakes, and I could no longer control that. This was not easy at all because I am a mother who loves to smother her kids. I had to let go and to let them grow up knowing that they are also children of God. God's love for them was evident.

> She openeth her mouth with wisdom; and in her tongue is the law of kindness. ... Her children arise up, and call her blessed; her husband also, and he praiseth her. (Proverbs 31:26, 28)

God gave me freedom to love again without restraint. This meant I didn't owe anyone anything but love them. God gave me a heart of flesh. I forgave the trespasses people had committed against me, because God had forgiven me of my trespasses.

> Owe no man anything, but to love one another: for he that loveth another hath fulfilled the law. (Romans 13:8)

> And forgive us our debts, as we forgive our debtors. (Matthew 6:12)

Printed in the United States
by Baker & Taylor Publisher Services